AF268431

   I have worked in Photography for over thirty five years in one
role or another , from Dark room tech , to Wedding and Portrait
Photographer and even as a Cruise Ship Phographer for many
years.

   In my travels to far flung shores around the world , always
seeking new images through that little rectangular window in
front of my eye, the obvious or famous landmarks and views are
easy to spot , but what is -- just around that corner or over that
next hill ?

   This is the thought that inspires me to record what is seen
every day with barely a passing glance in the rush to go about our
daily life .

   I am lucky to be living on this beautifull Island off the Atlantic
coast of Canada for the past seventeen years .
Prince Edward Island

Wandering Through my Lens
By
Richard W J Conyard

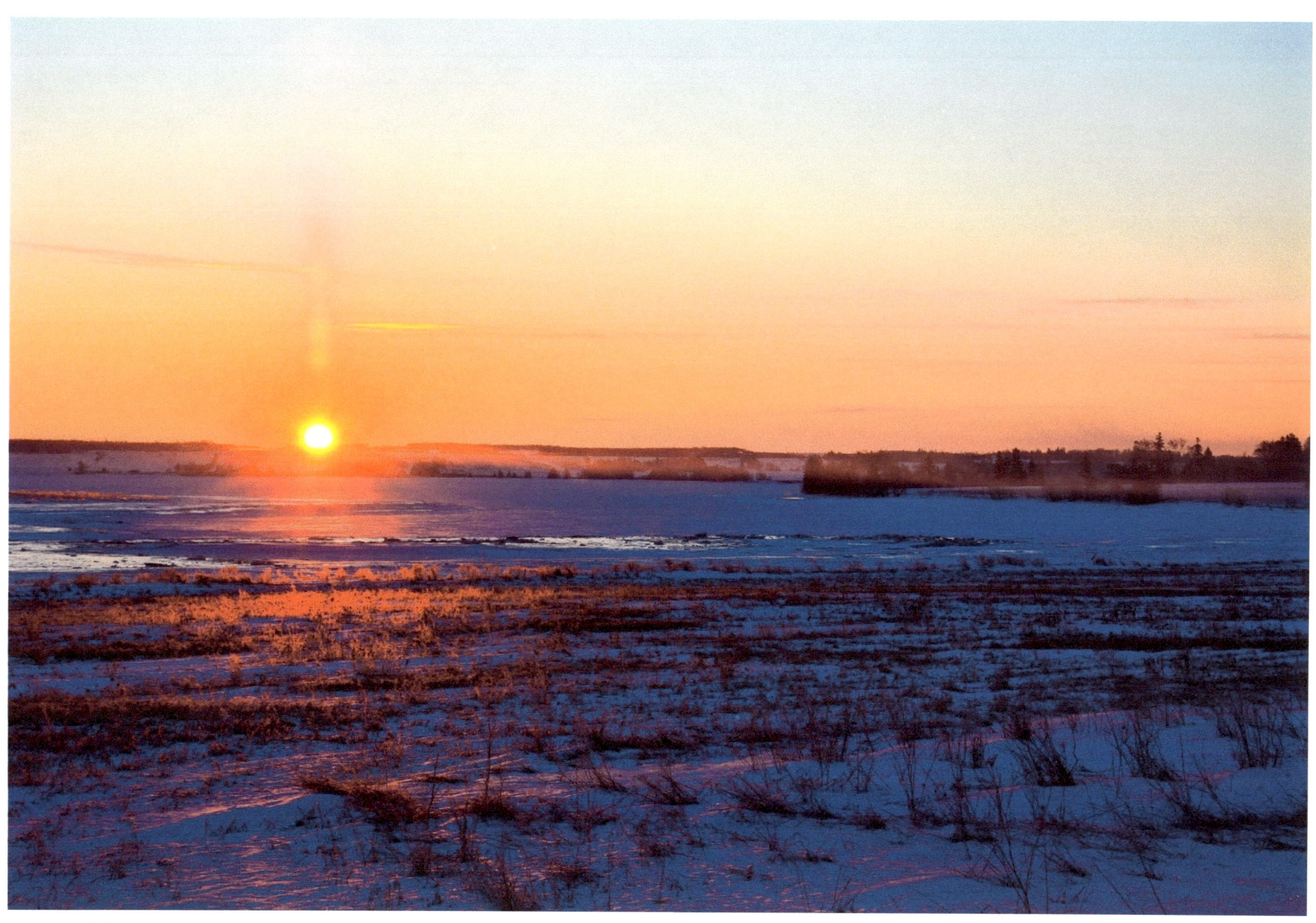

Beautiful Sunsets on a beautiful Island.

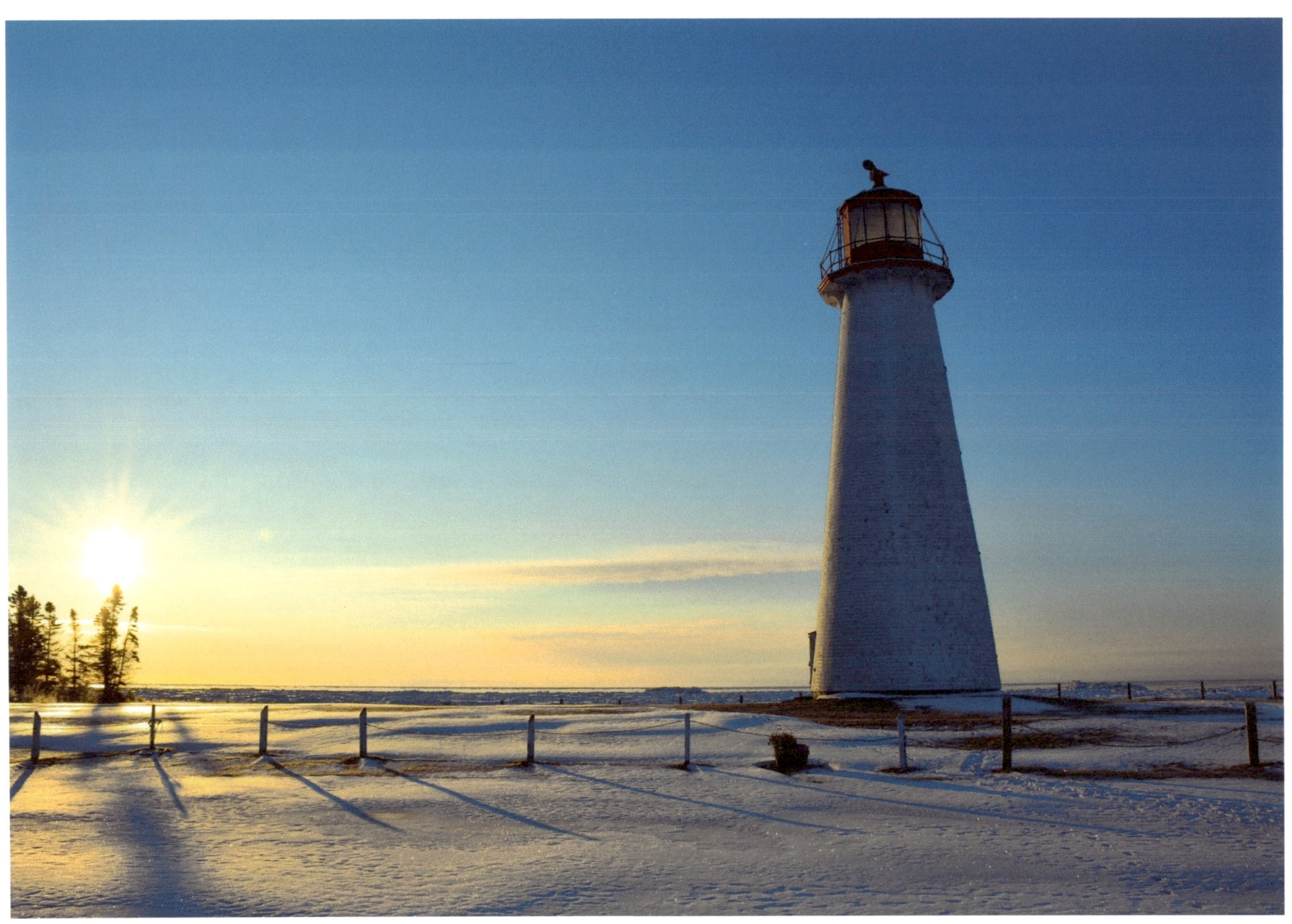

Point Prim Lighthouse.

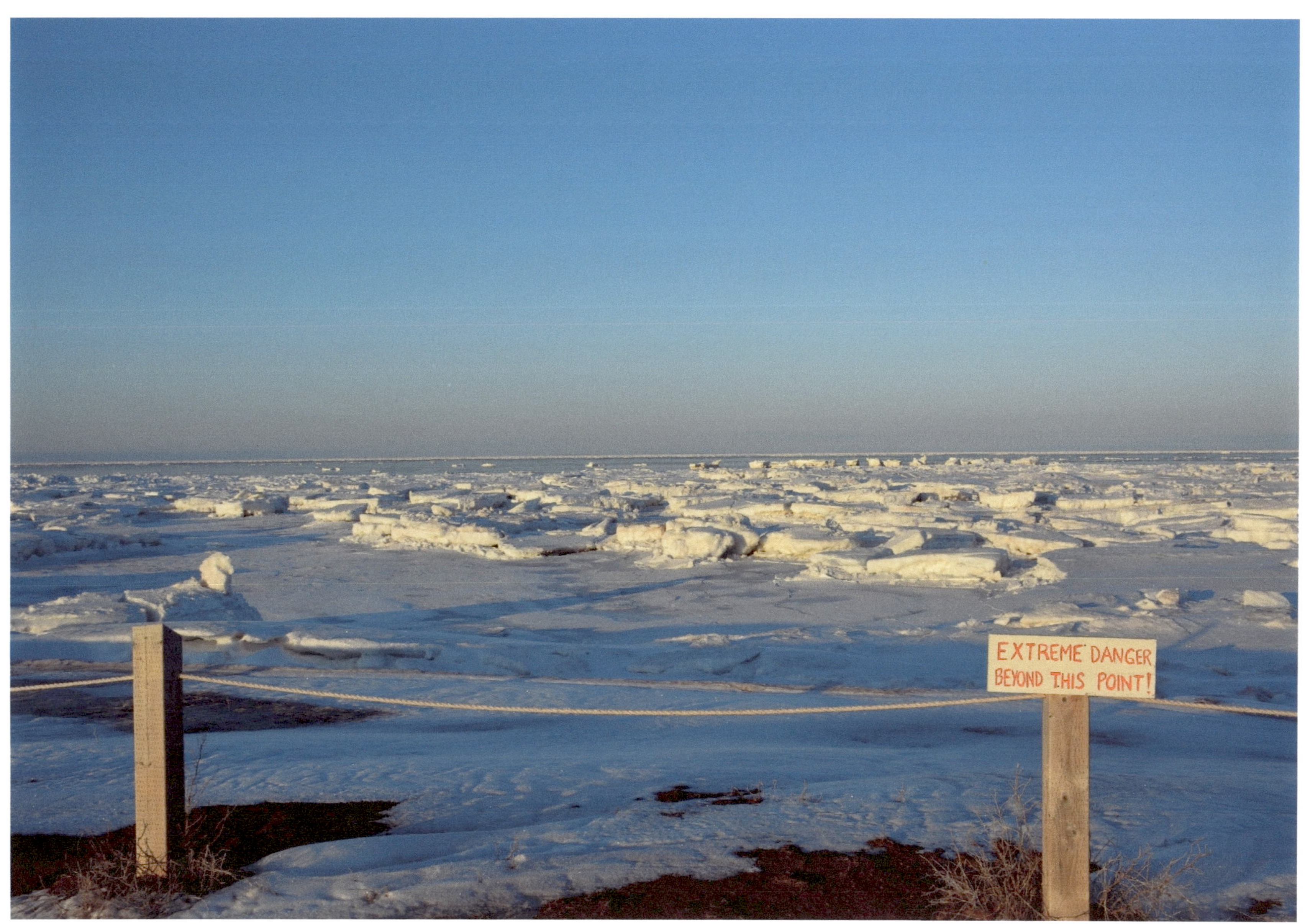

Frozen shore of the Northumberland Straight from Point Prim.

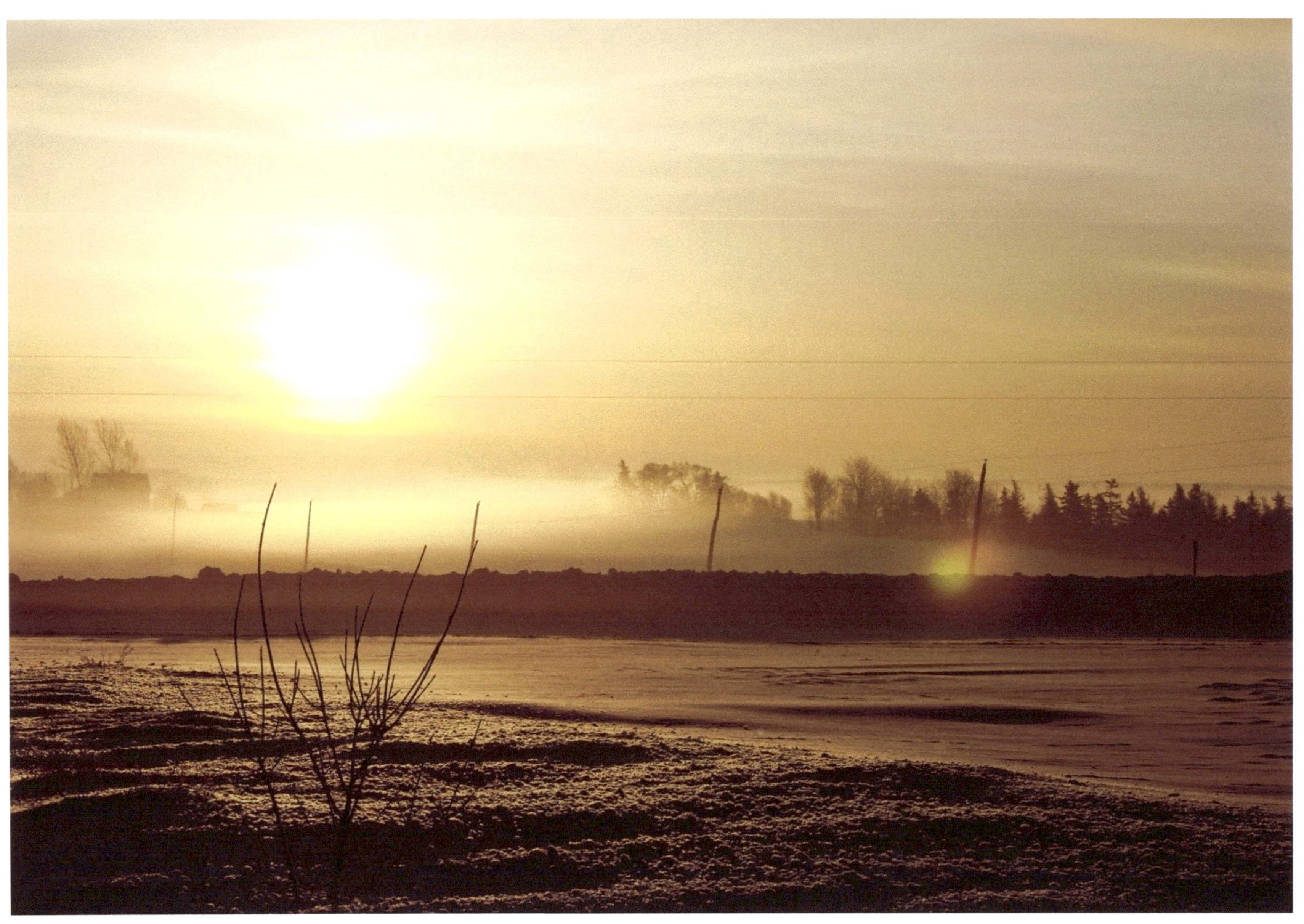

The morning after a blizzard.

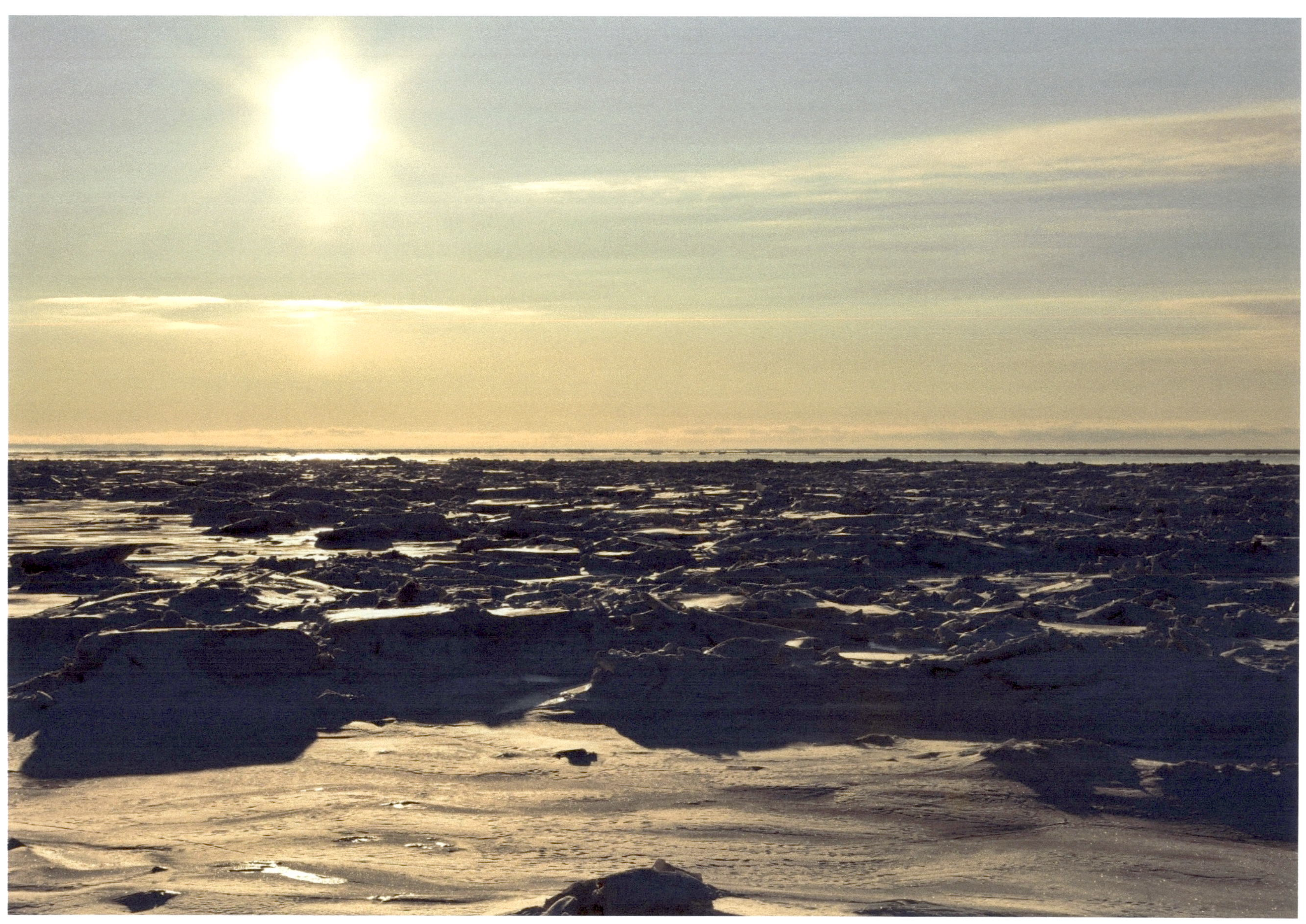

Frozen shore.

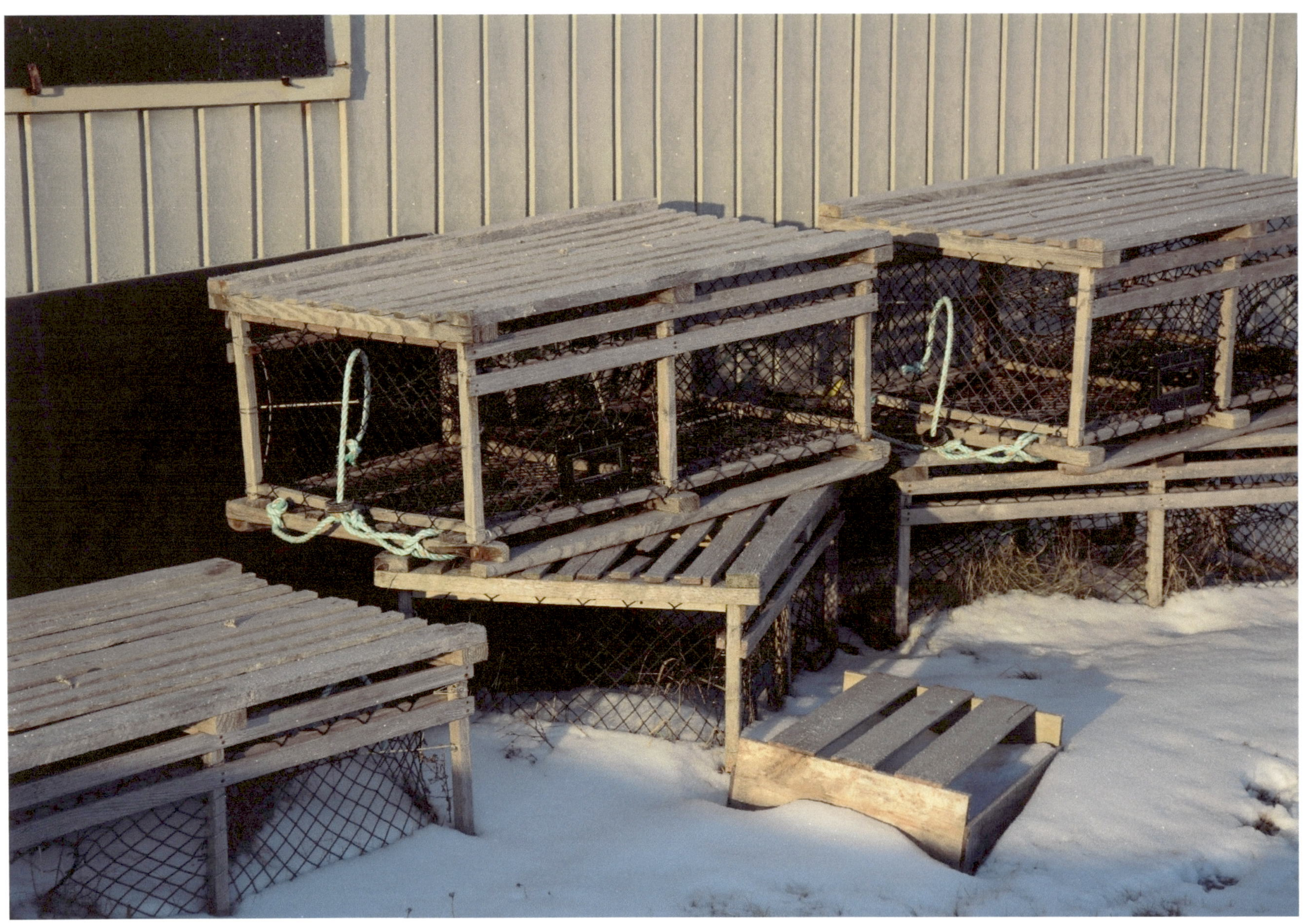

Lobster traps

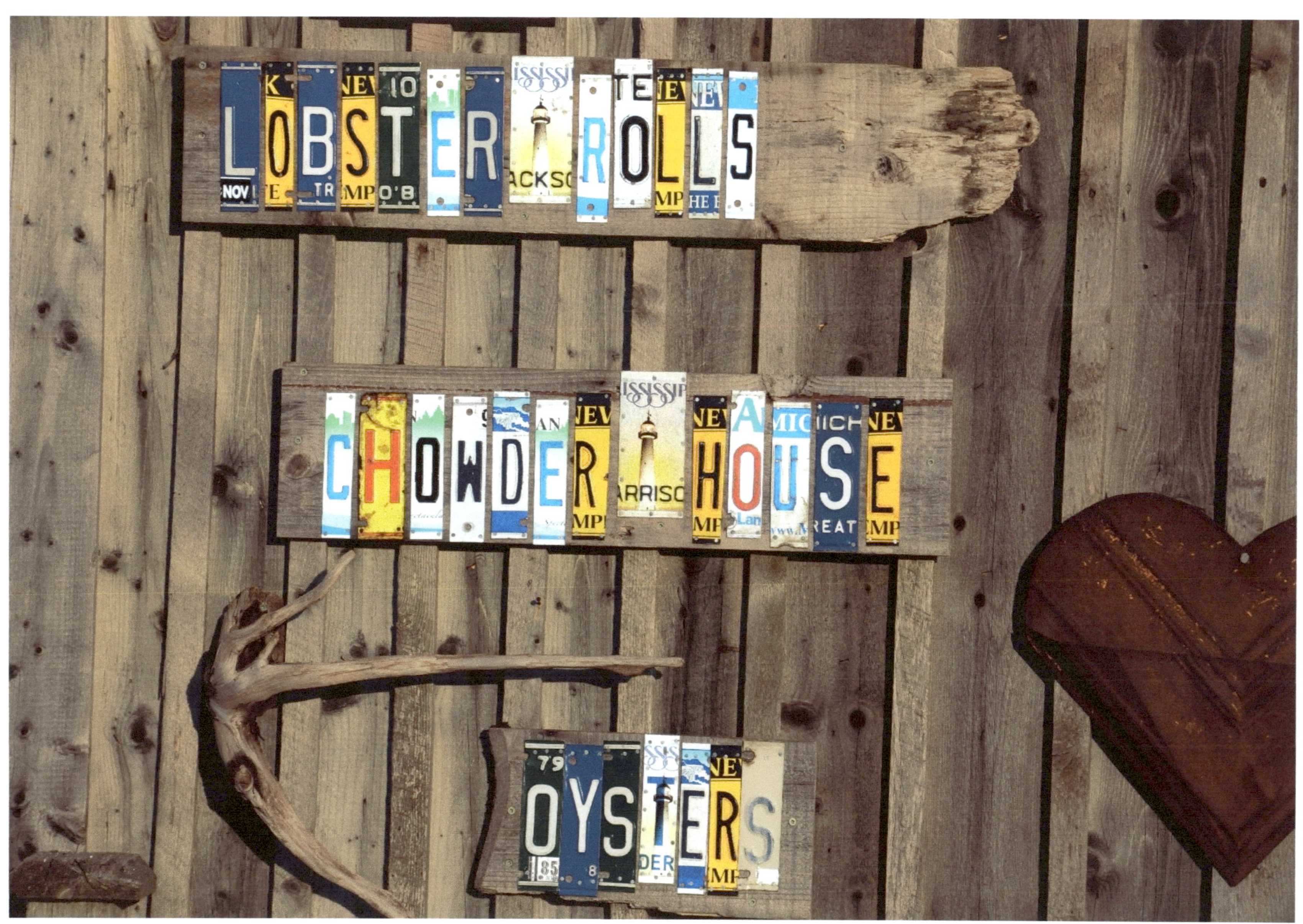

Creative sign Point Prim.

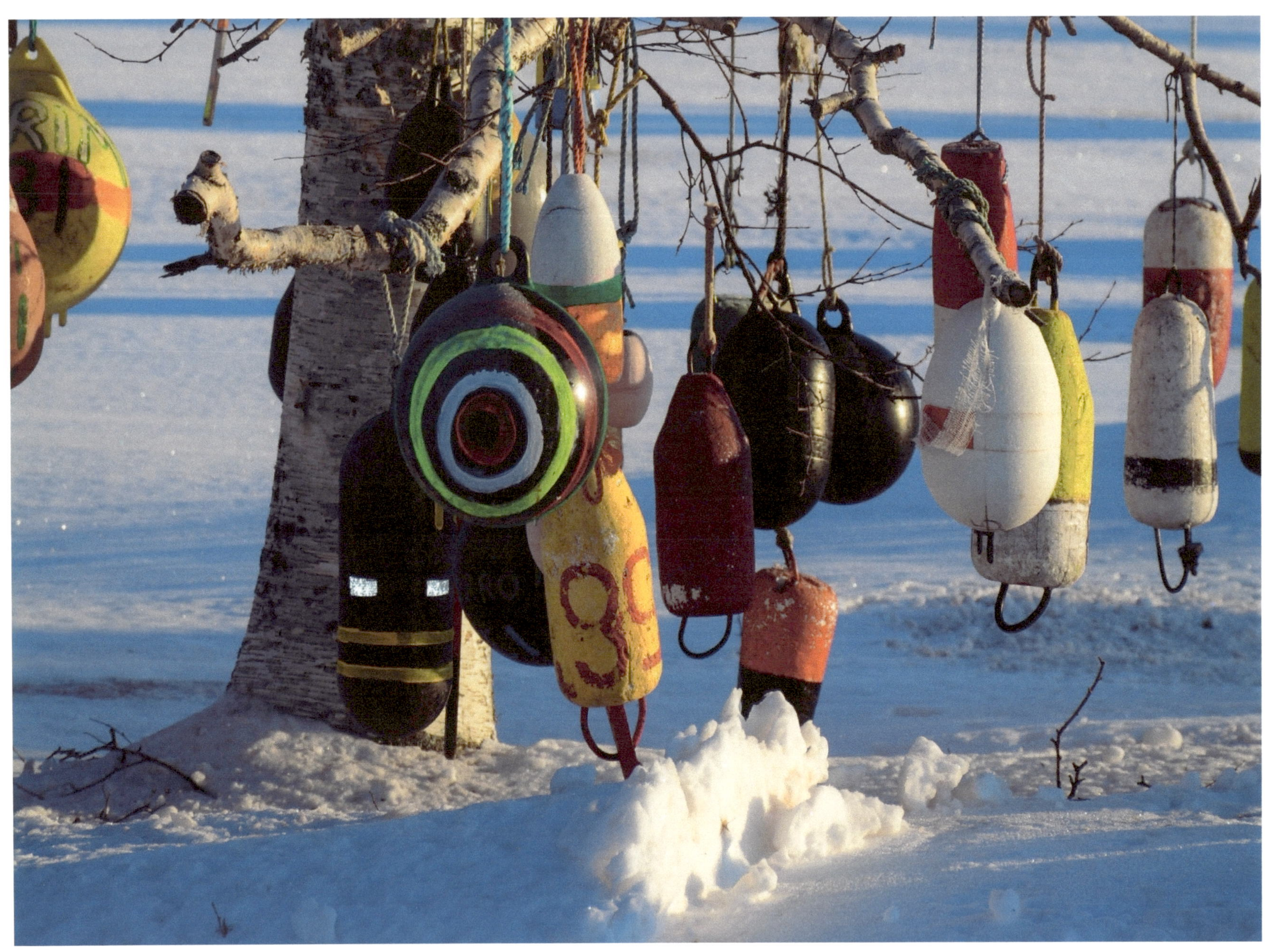

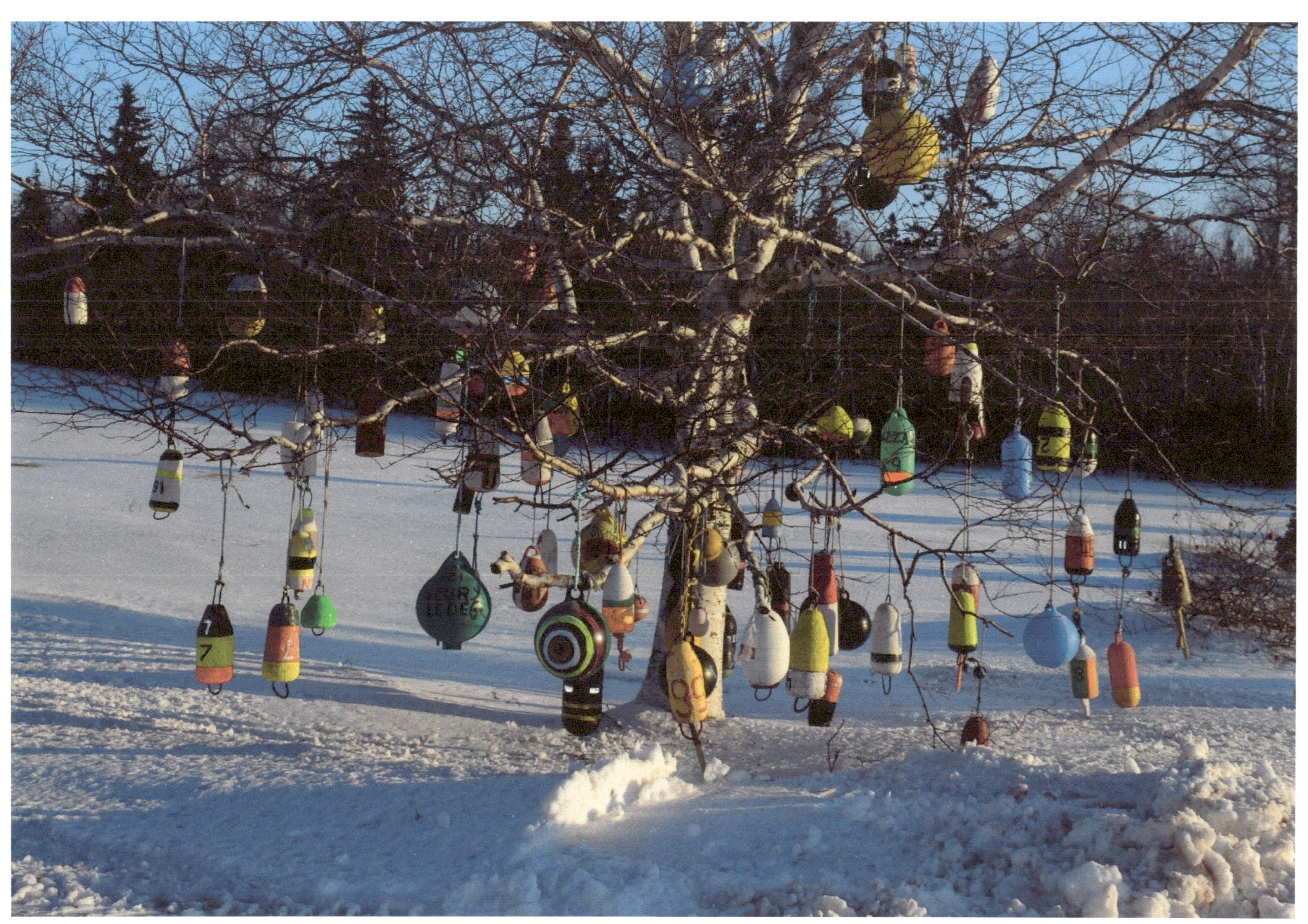

The fishing buoy tree near Point Prim.

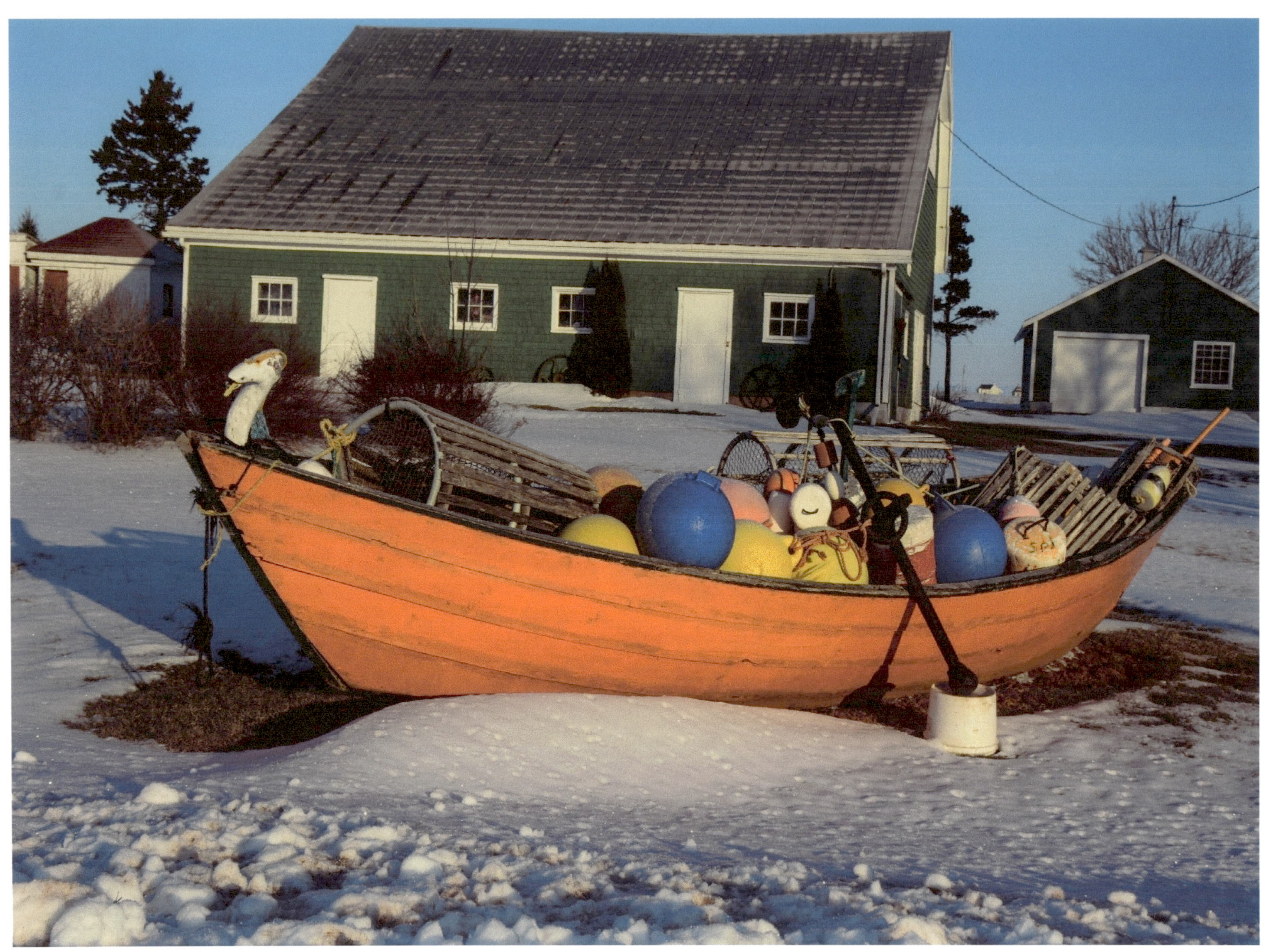

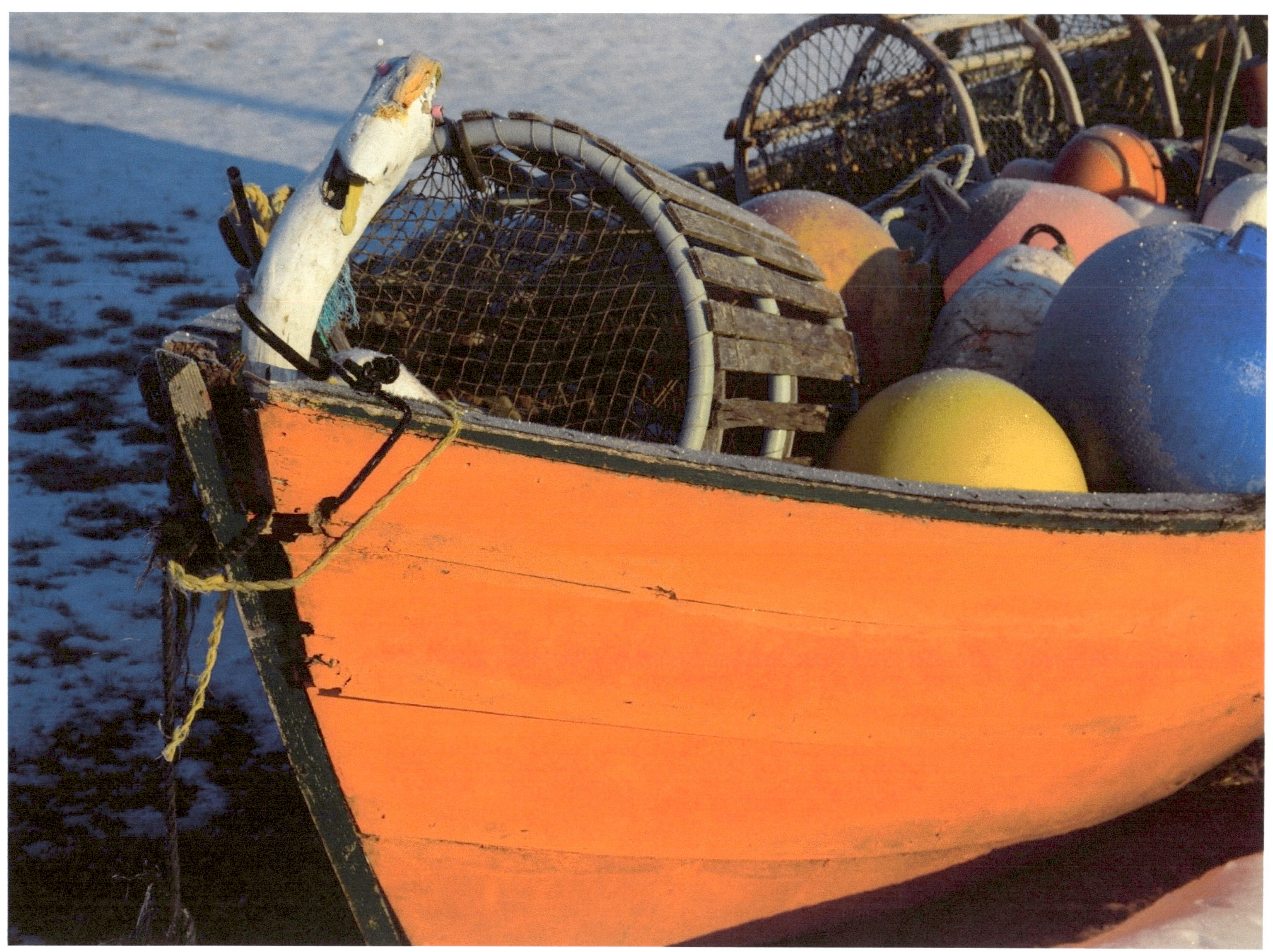

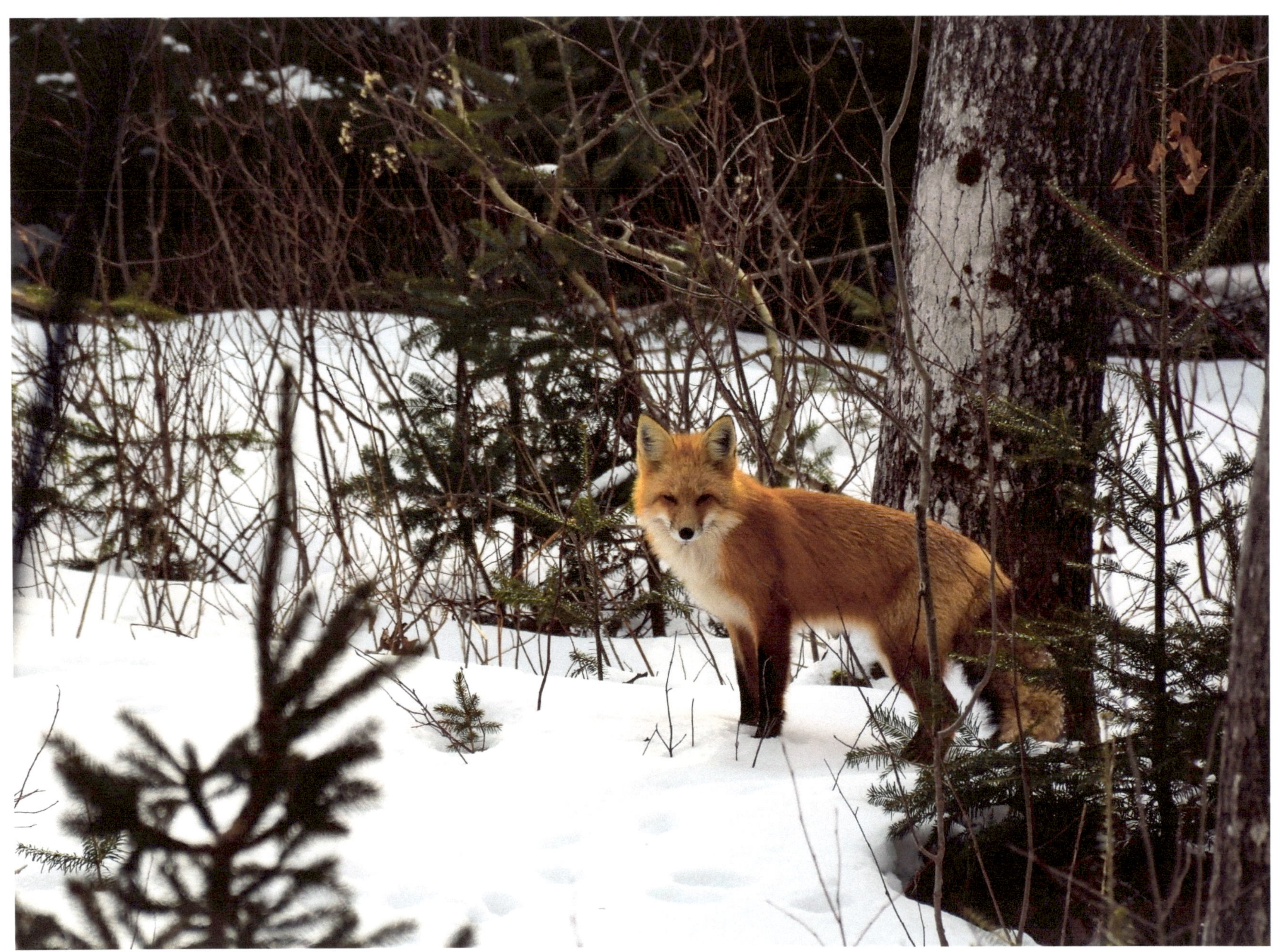

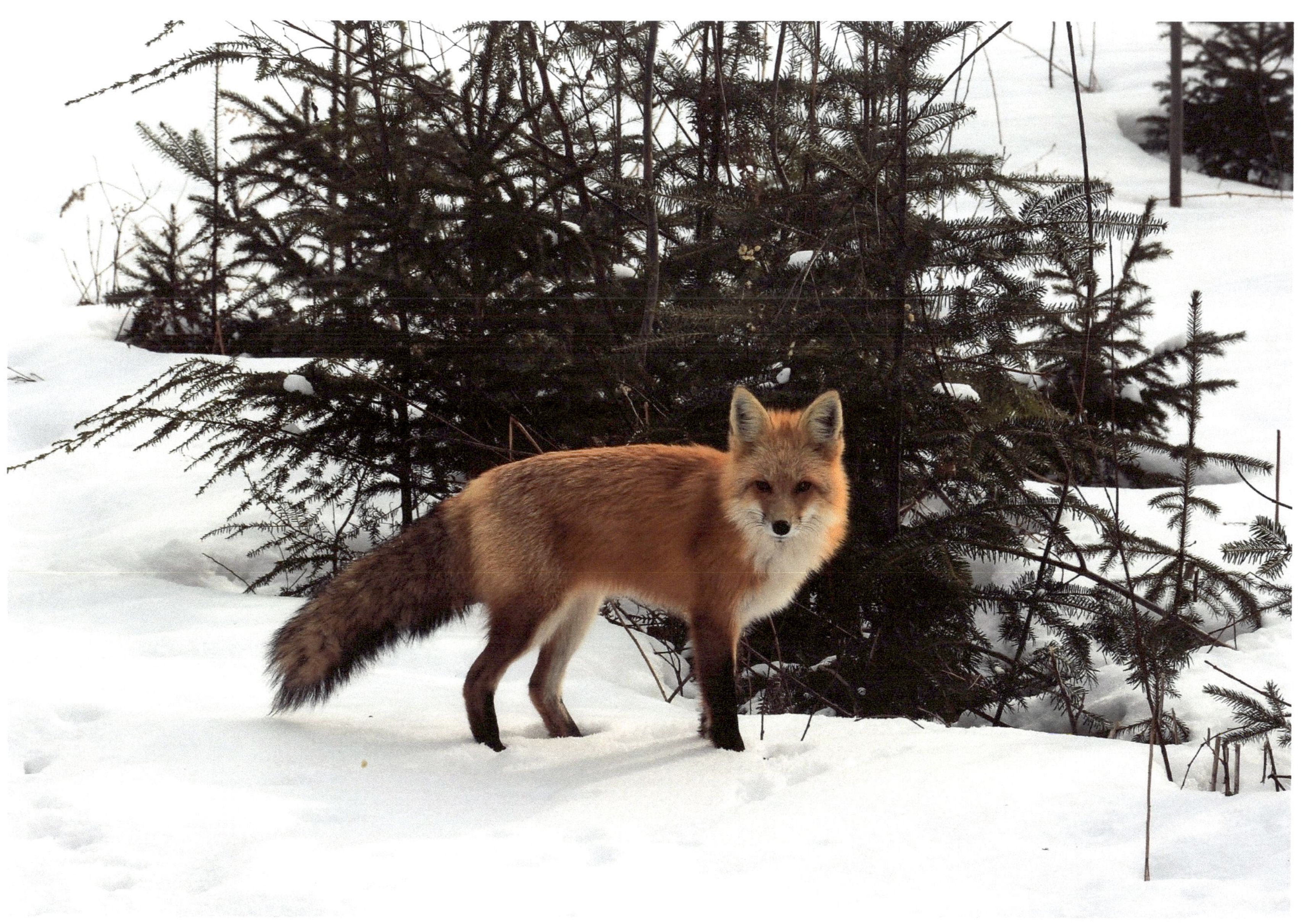

Early visitor for breakfast.

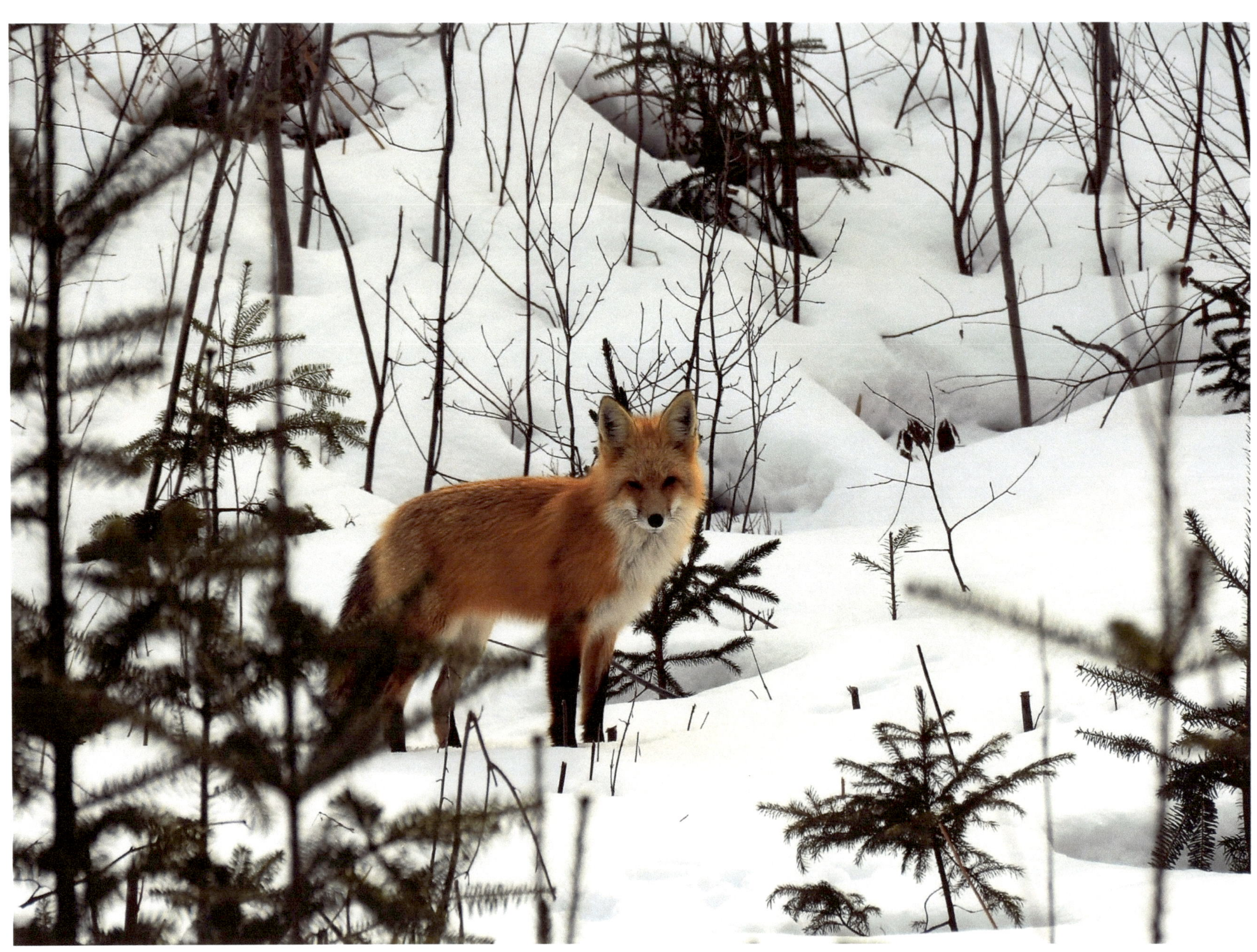

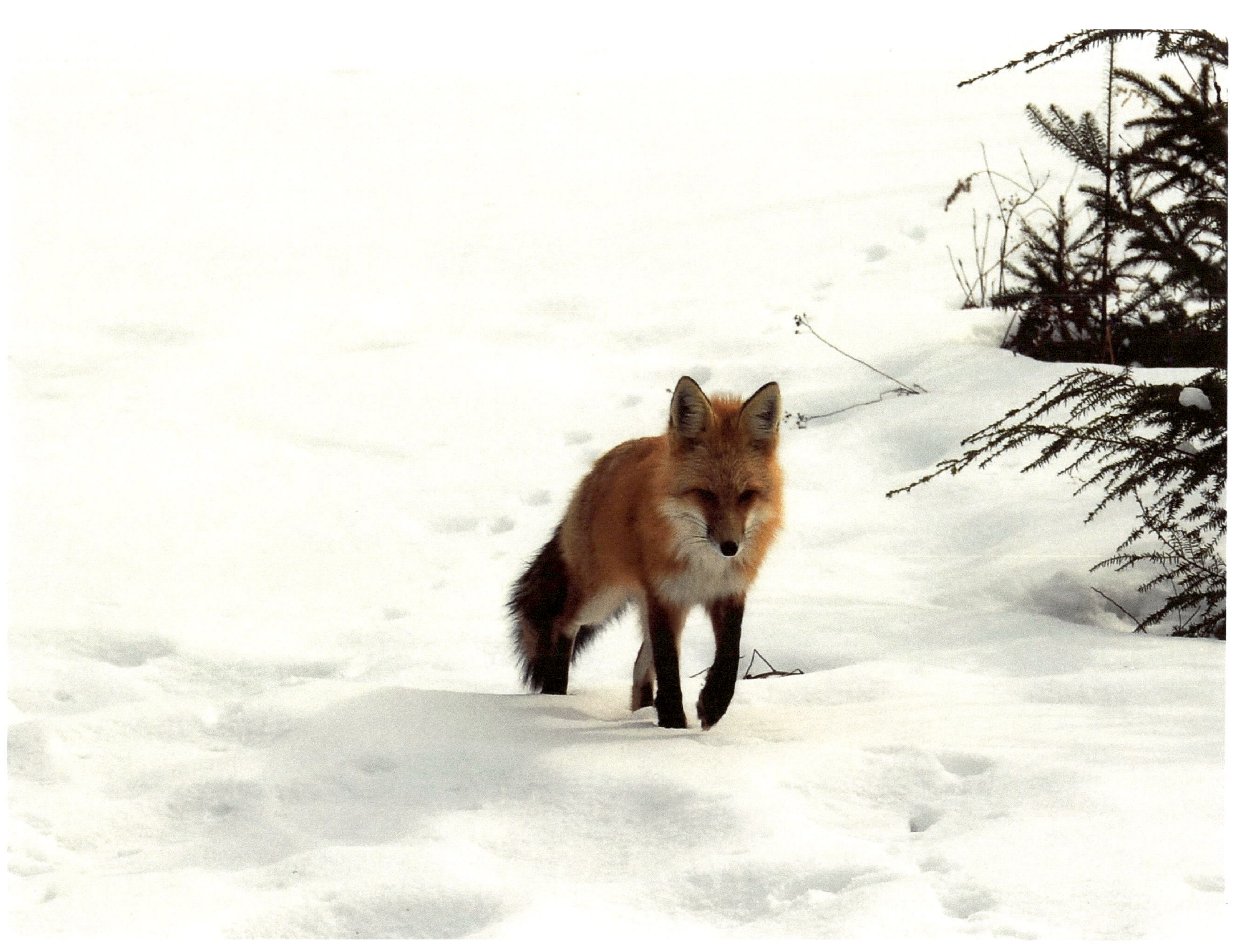

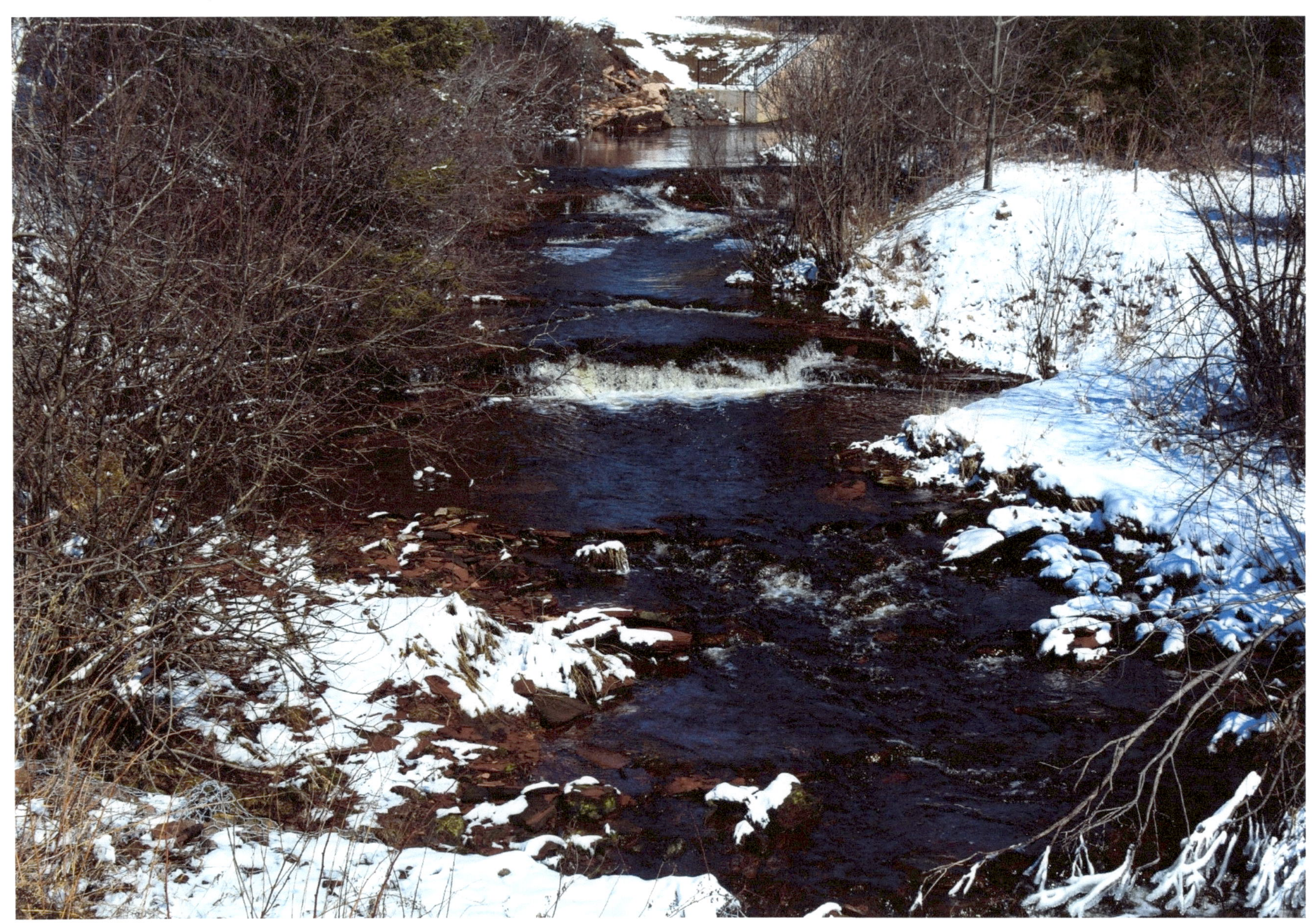

Fish ladder at Vernon River, very popular fishing spot with locals .

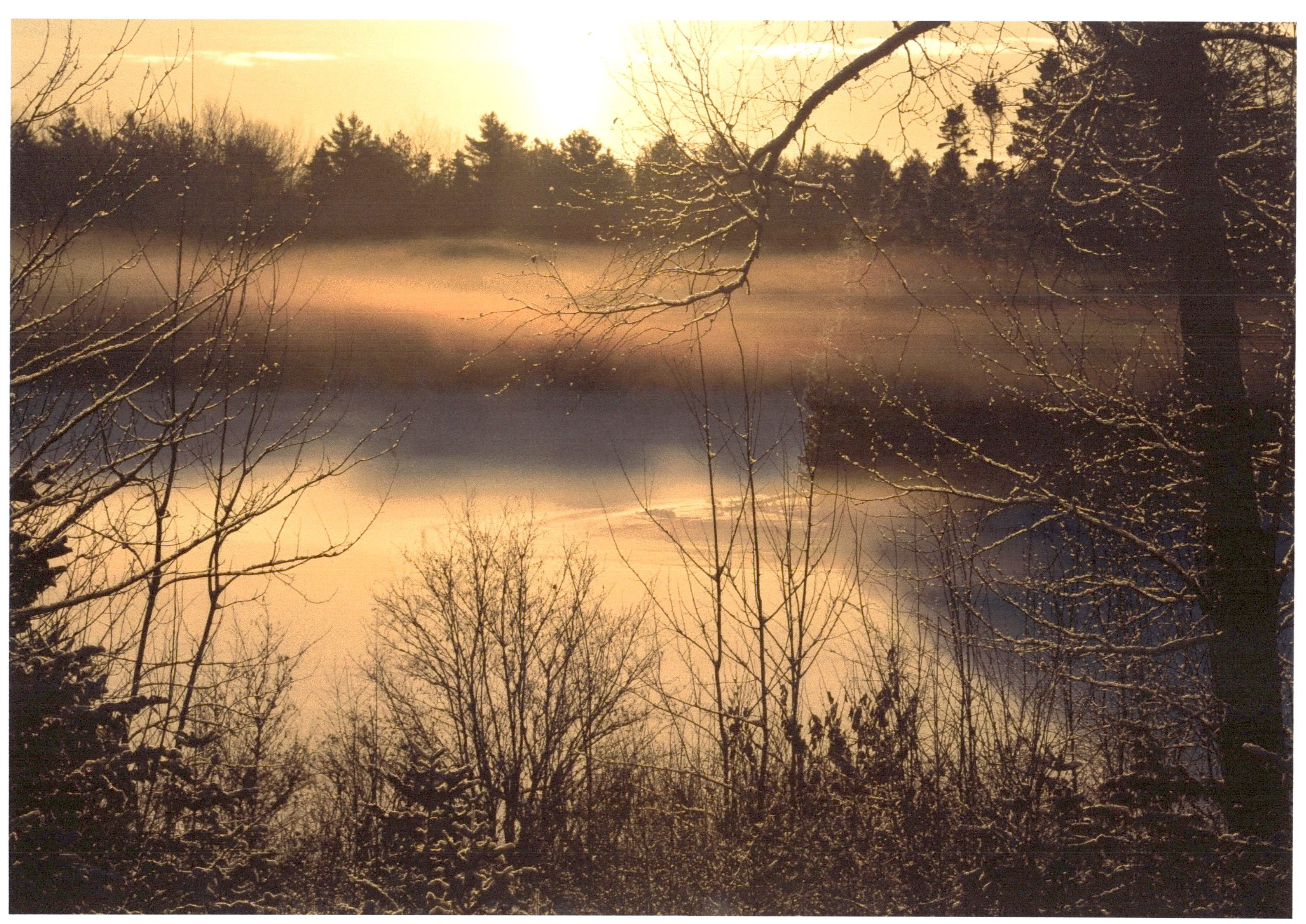

Early morning mists , Cahoon's Wharf.

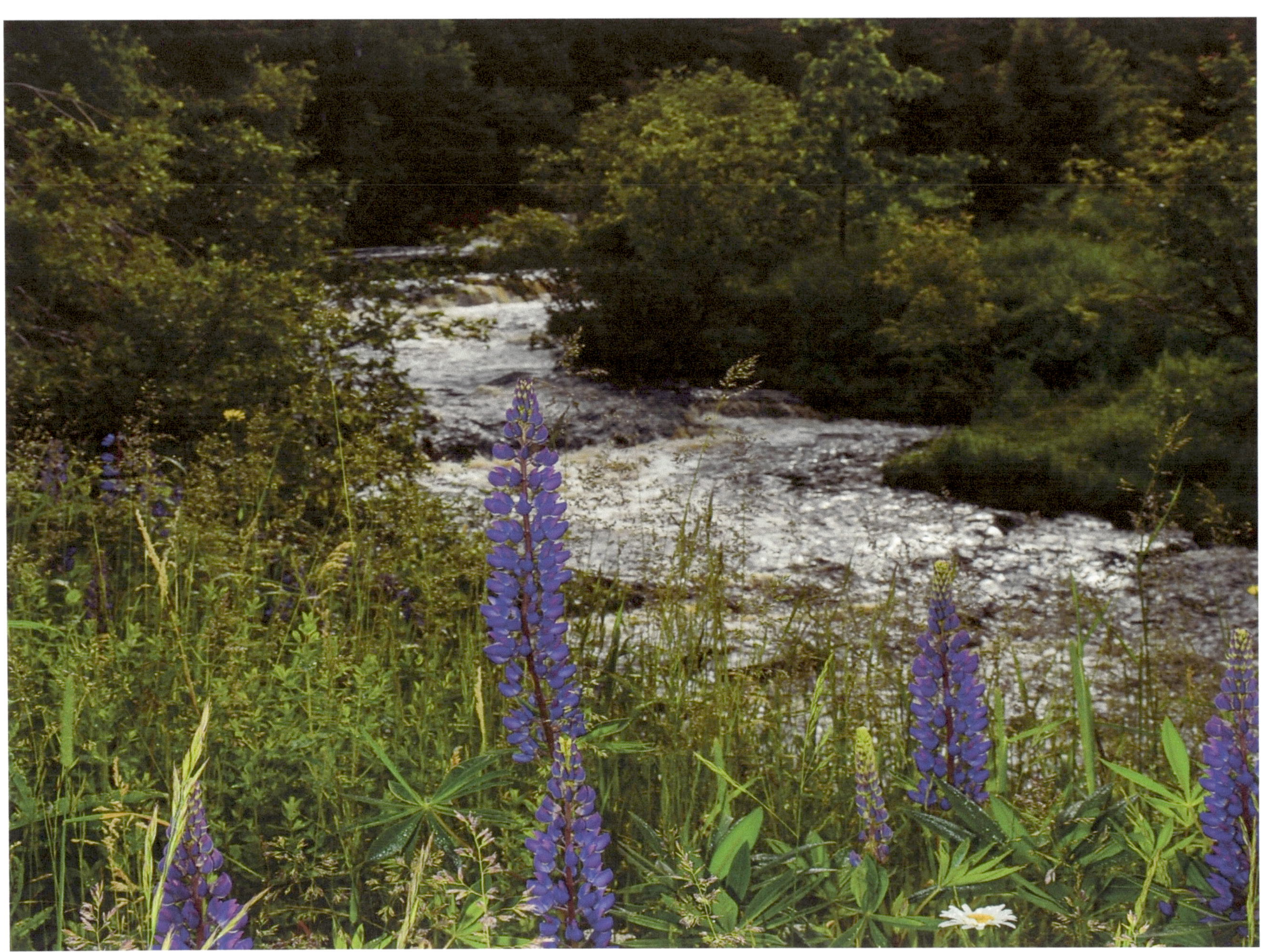

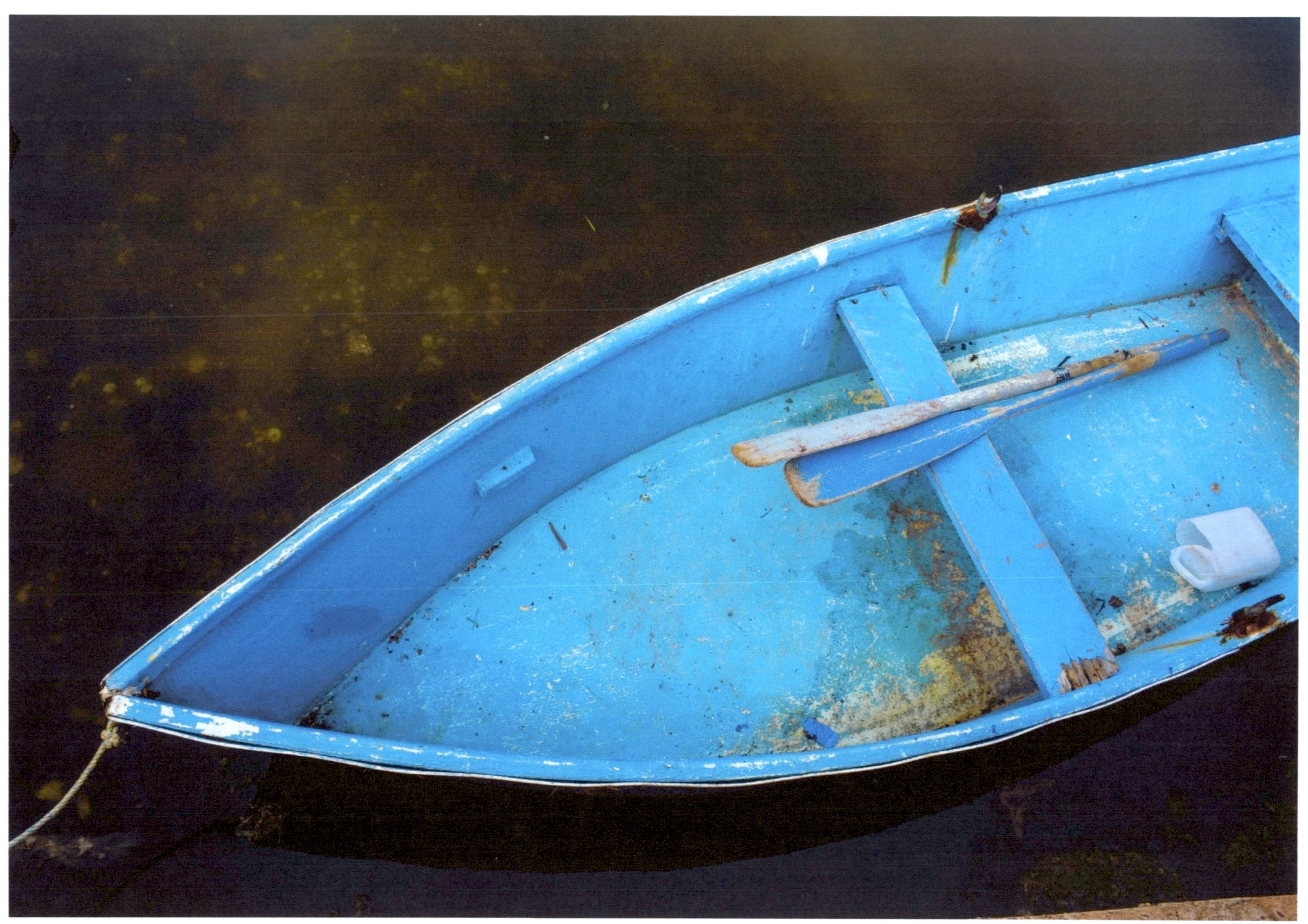

The blue boat.

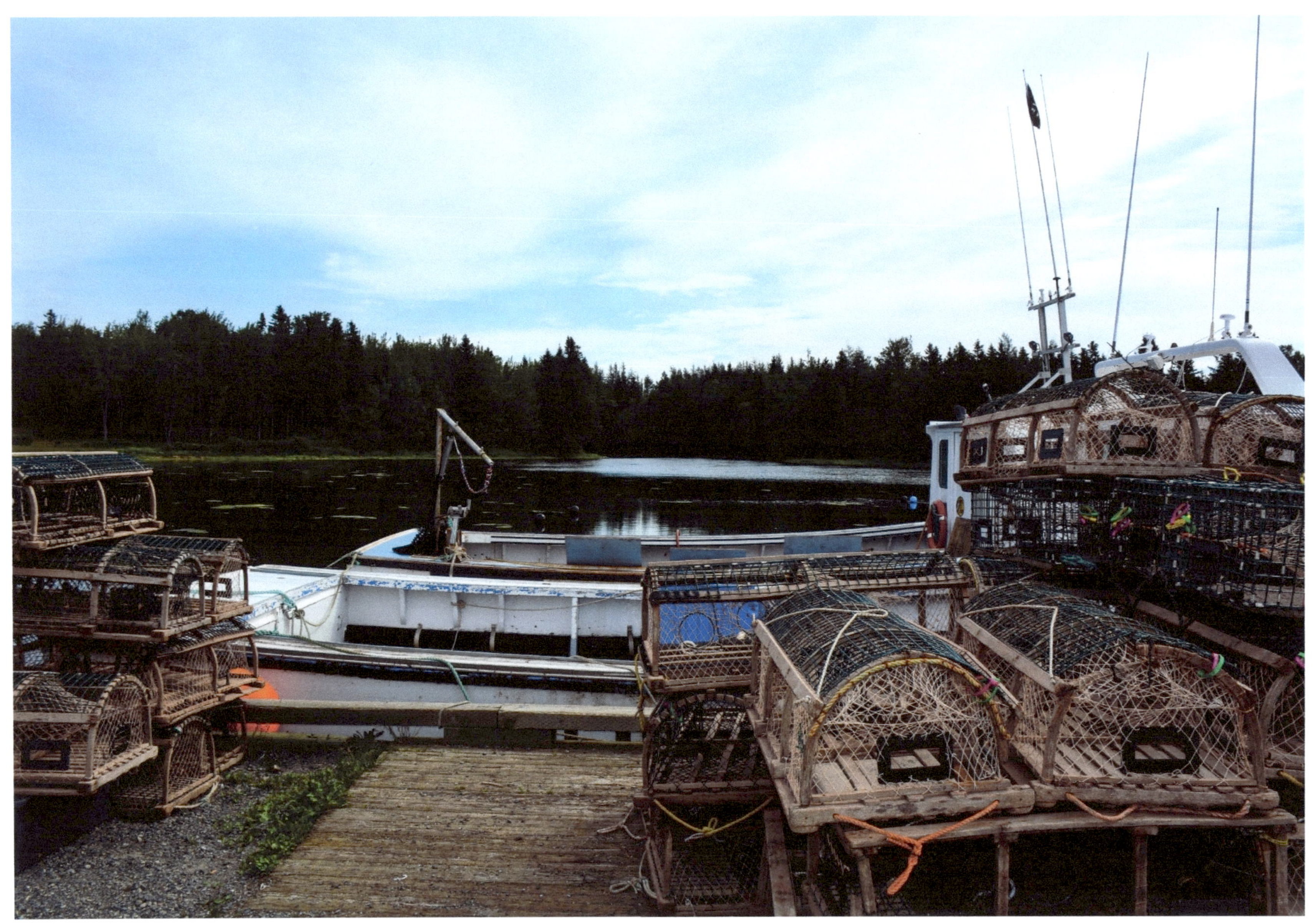

Traps ready to load, Cahoon's Wharf.

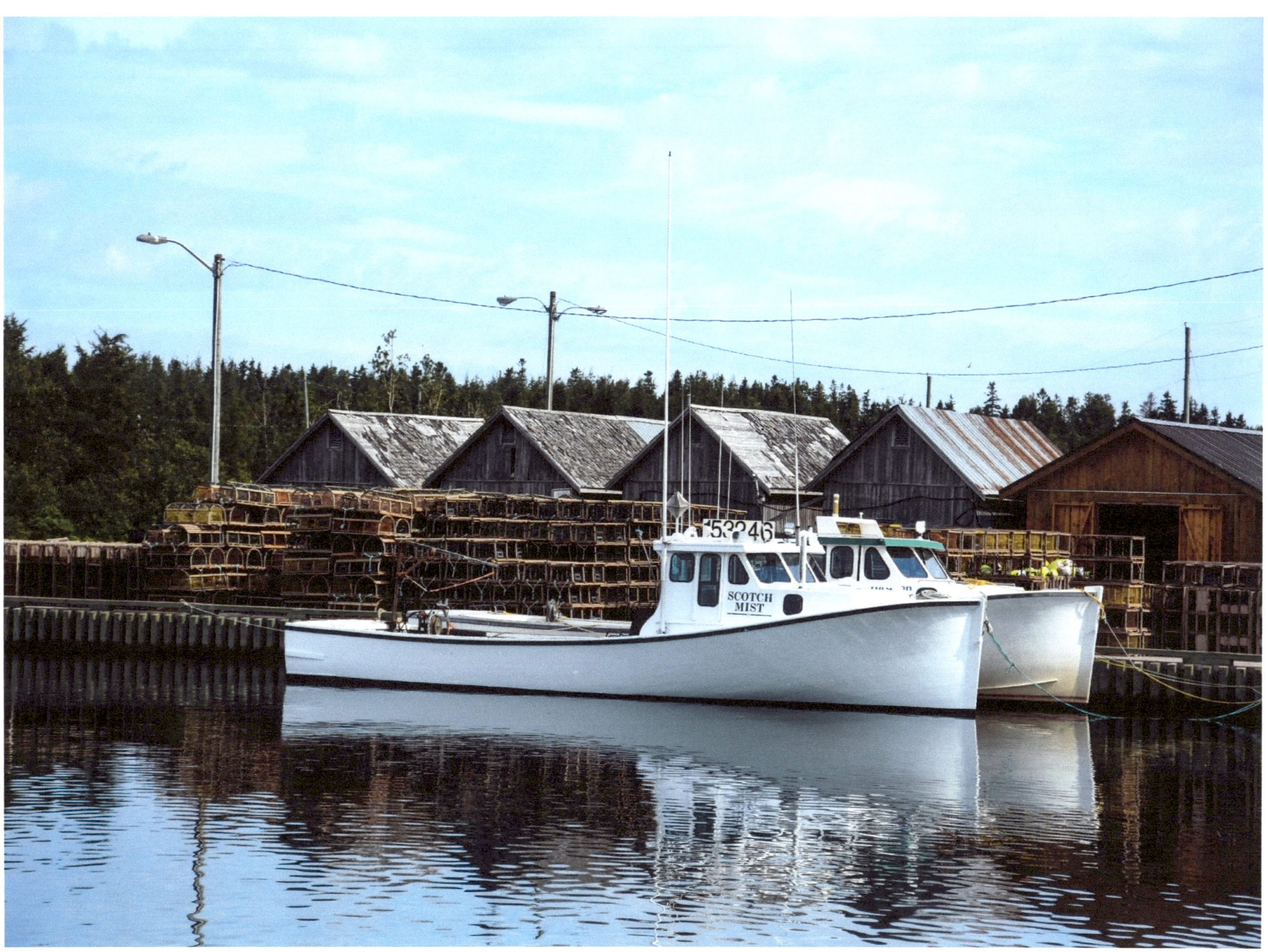
153246
SCOTCH
MIST

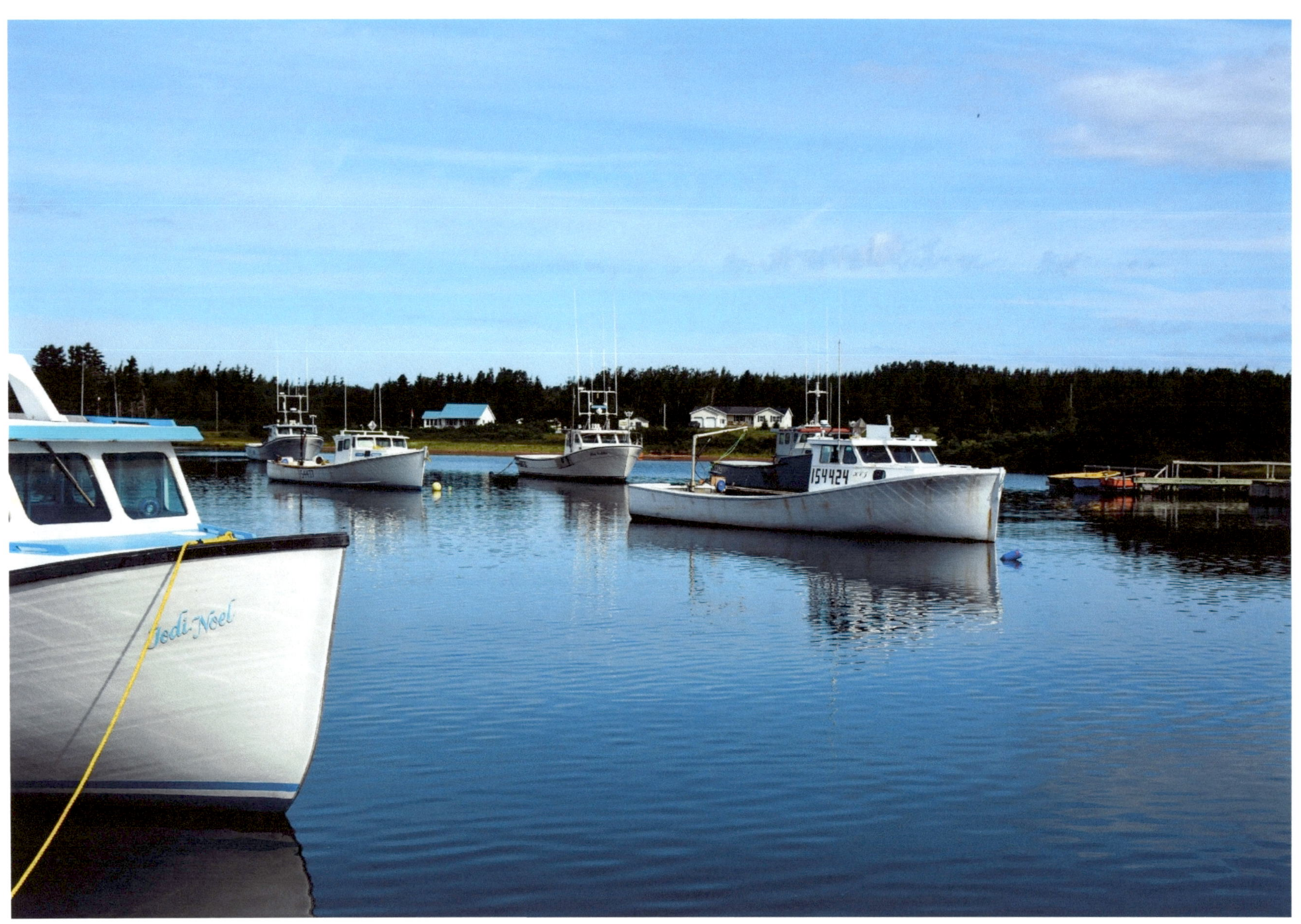

Grahams Pond and Wharf.

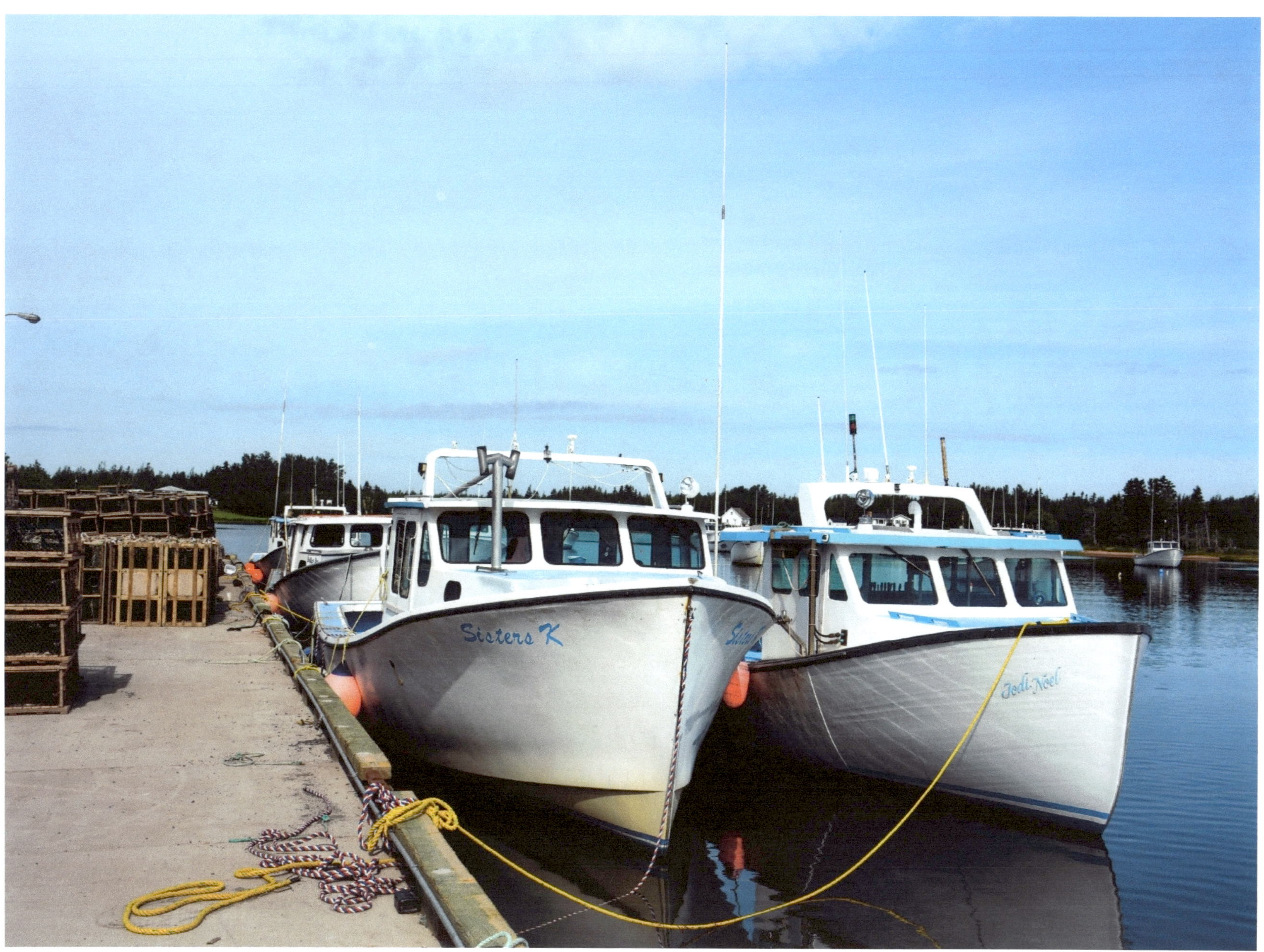

Sisters K
Jodi-Noel

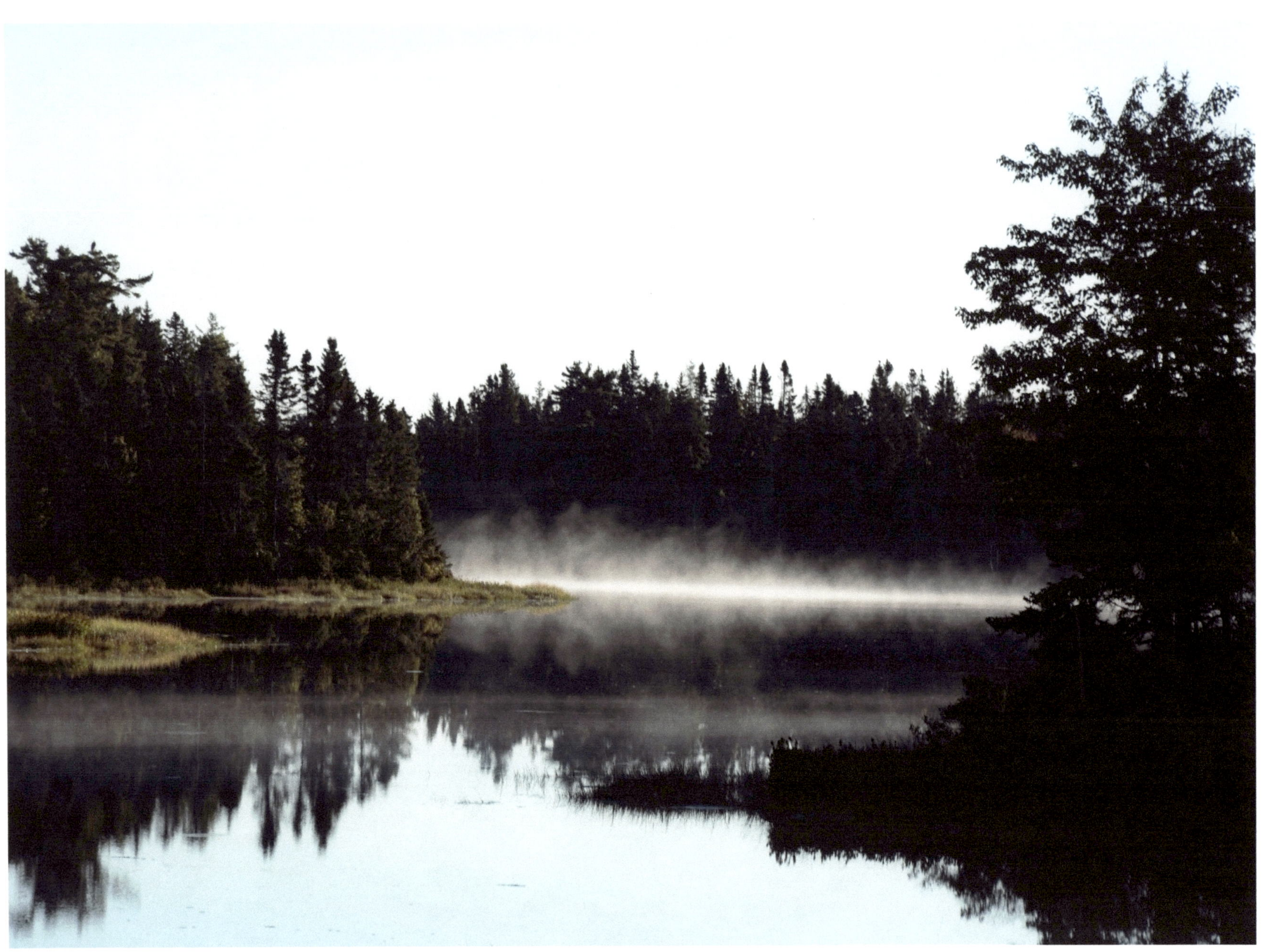

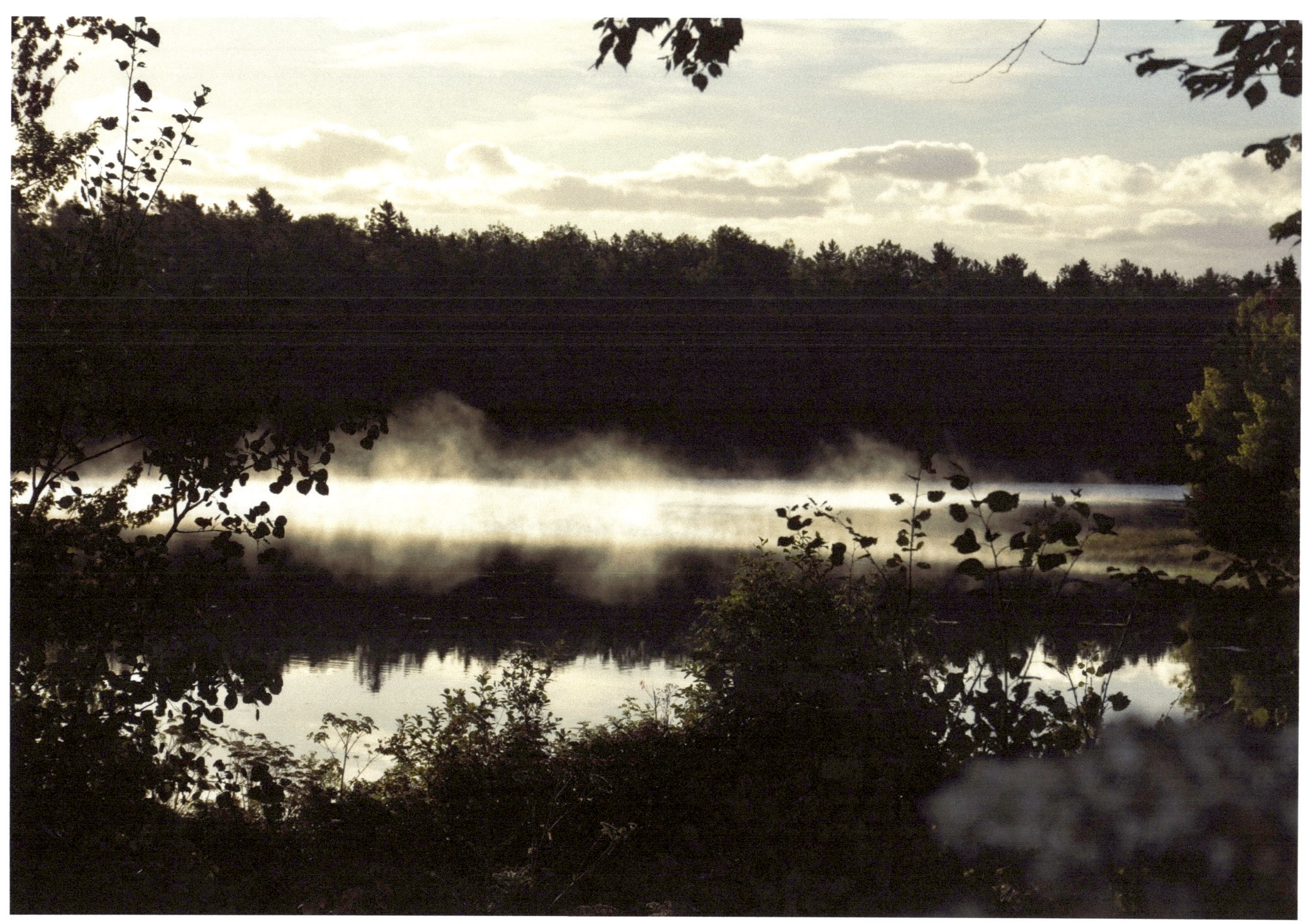

Misty mornings.

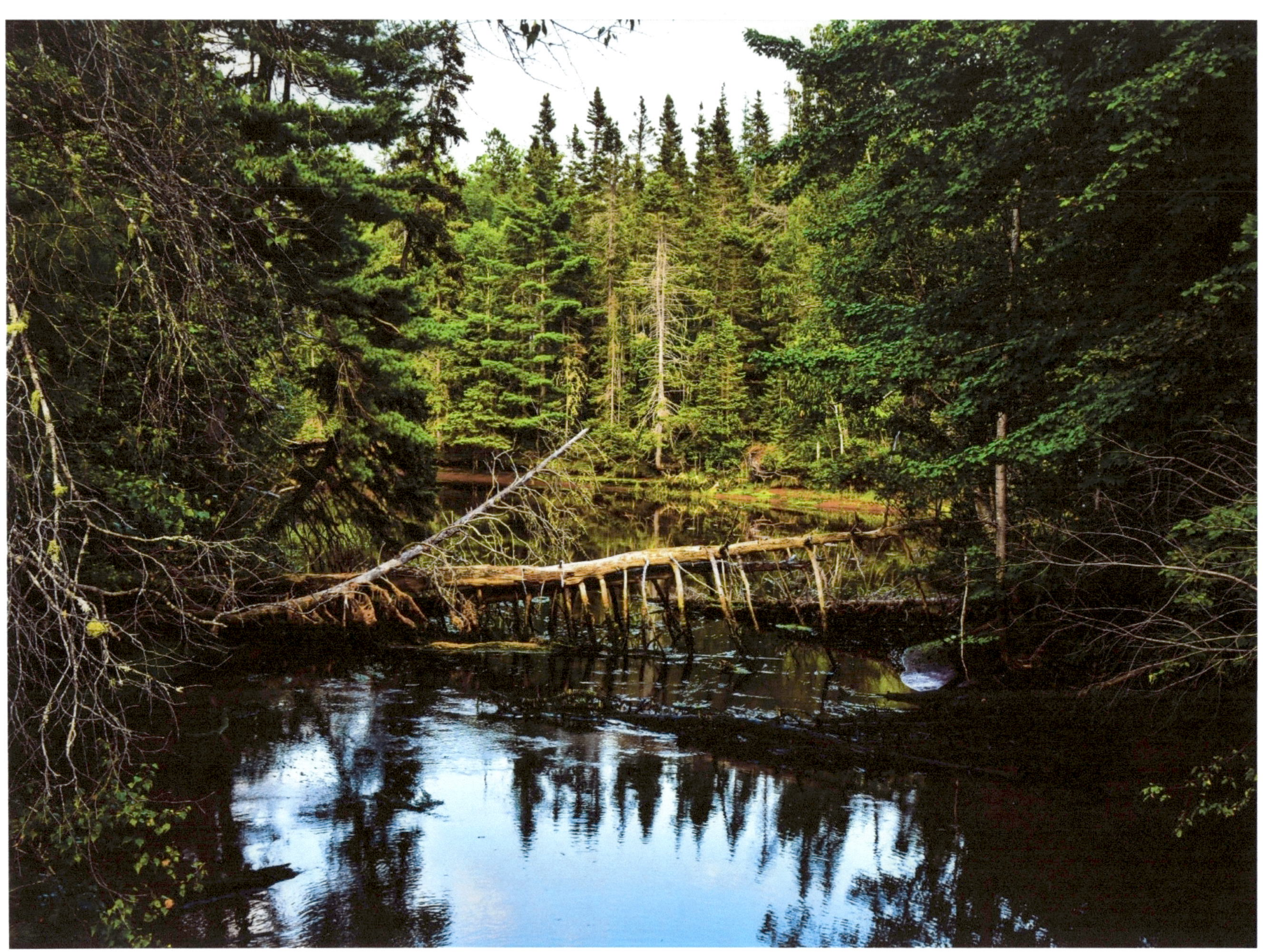

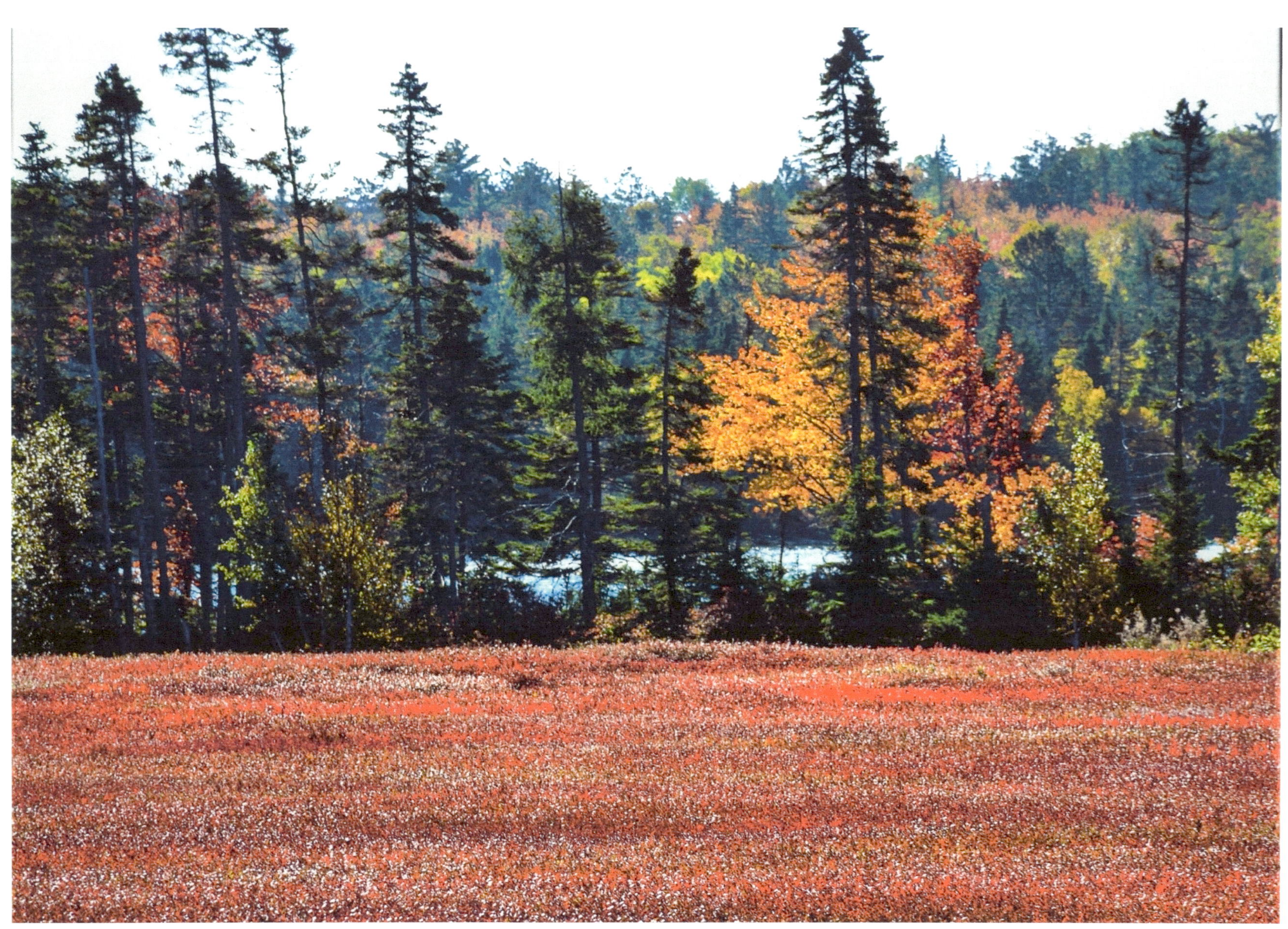

Blue Berry fields, Greek River.

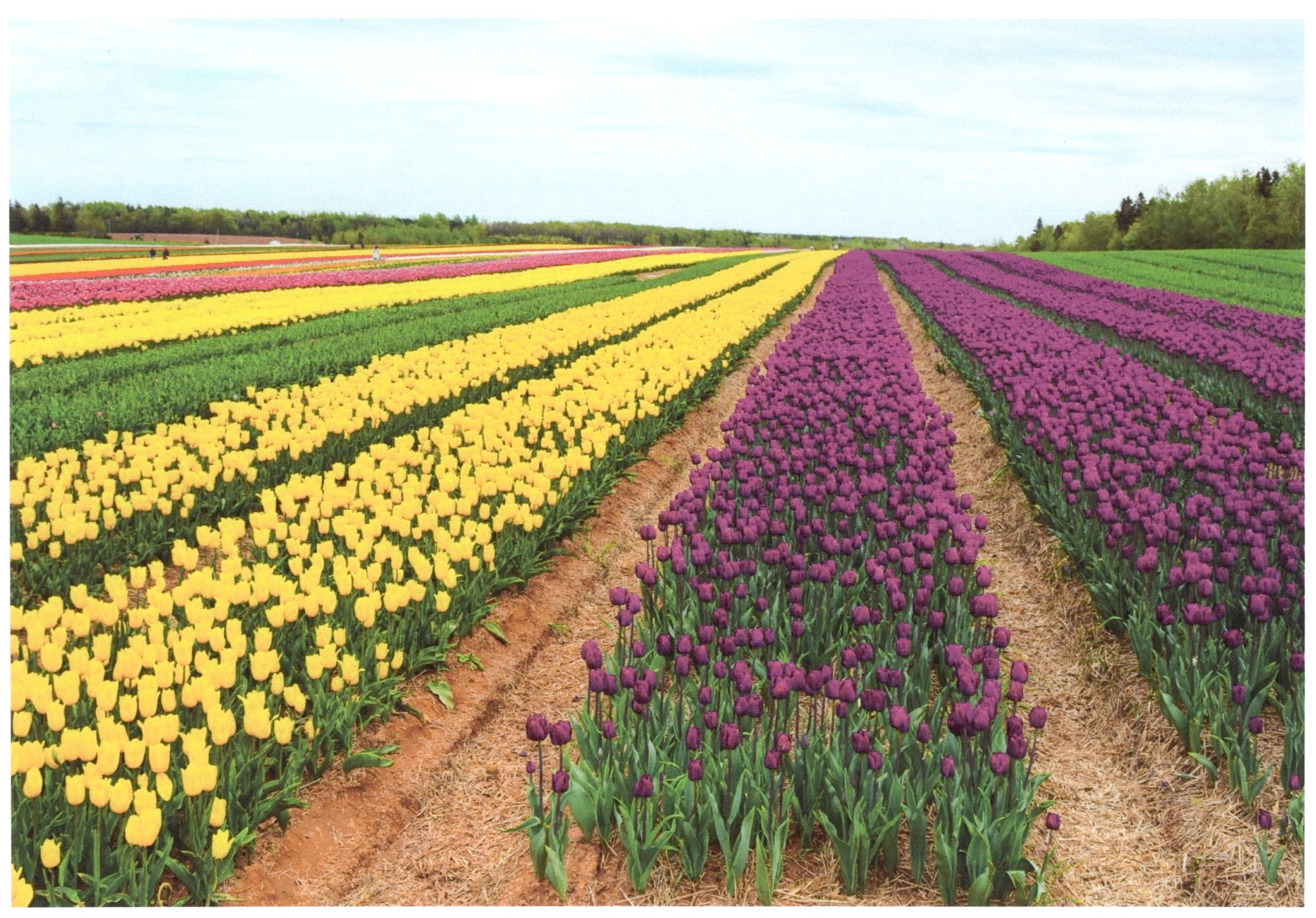

Tulip fields can be spotted in many places around the Island and add a vivid splash of colour in contrast to the lush greens .

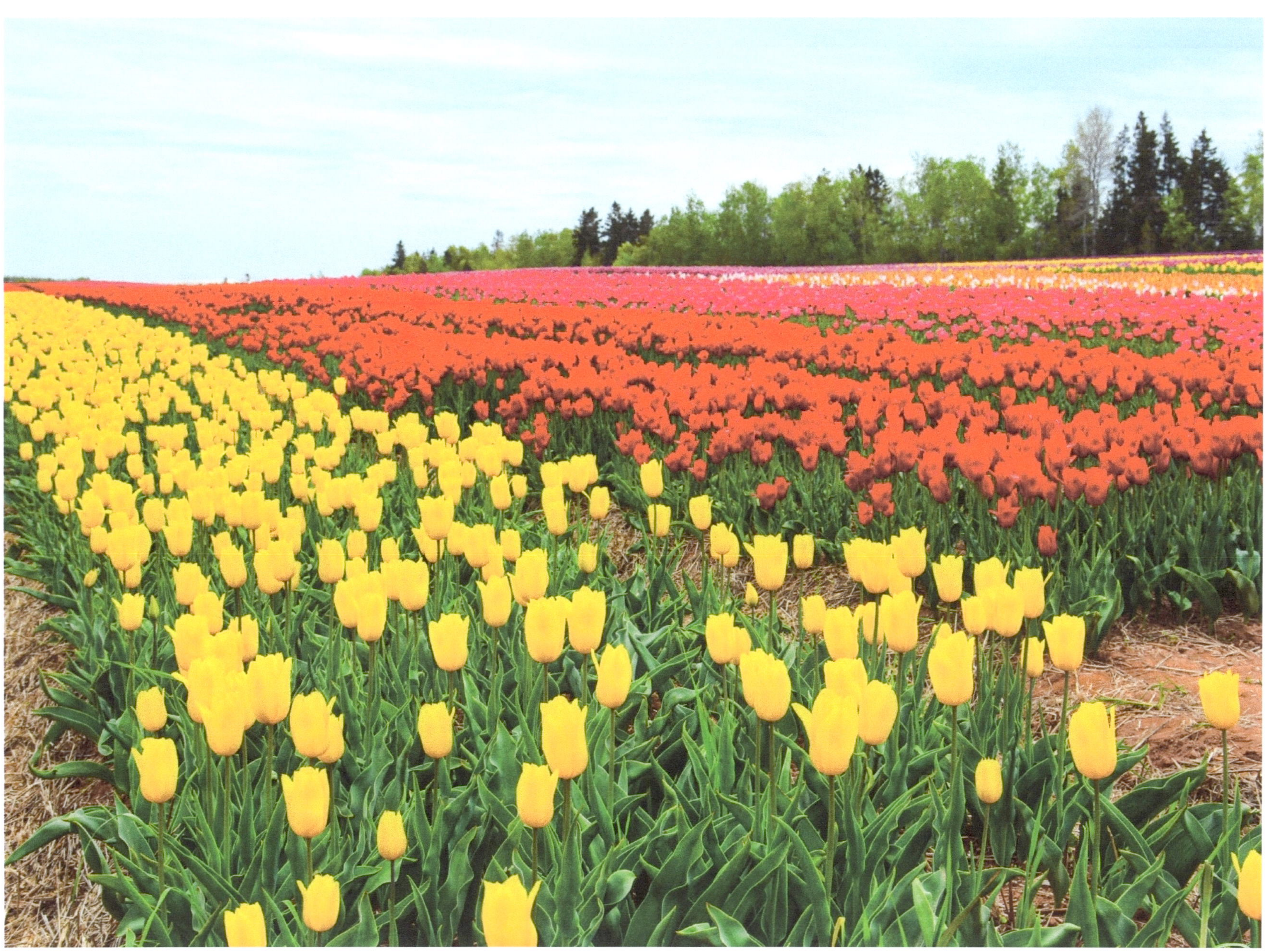

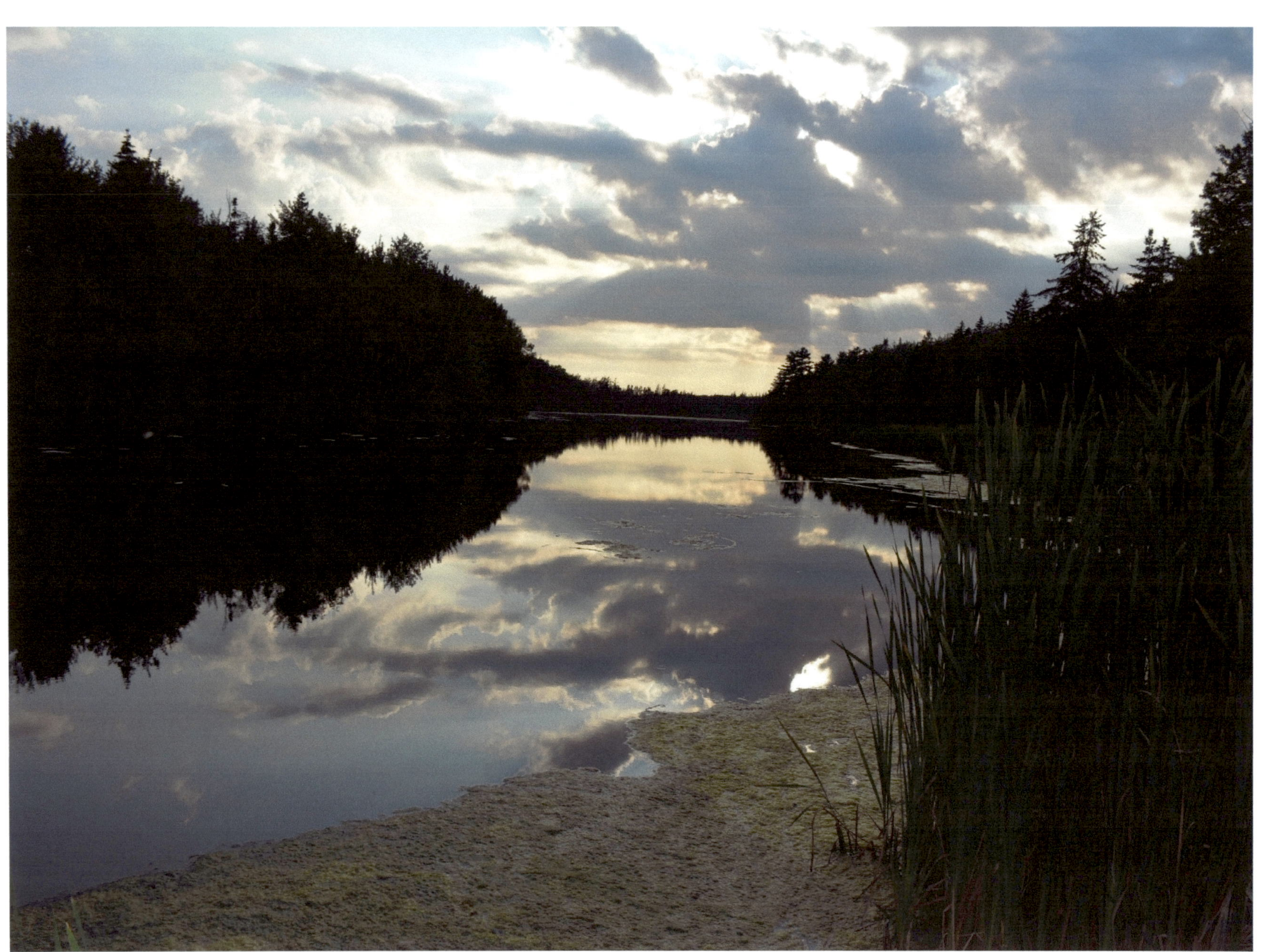

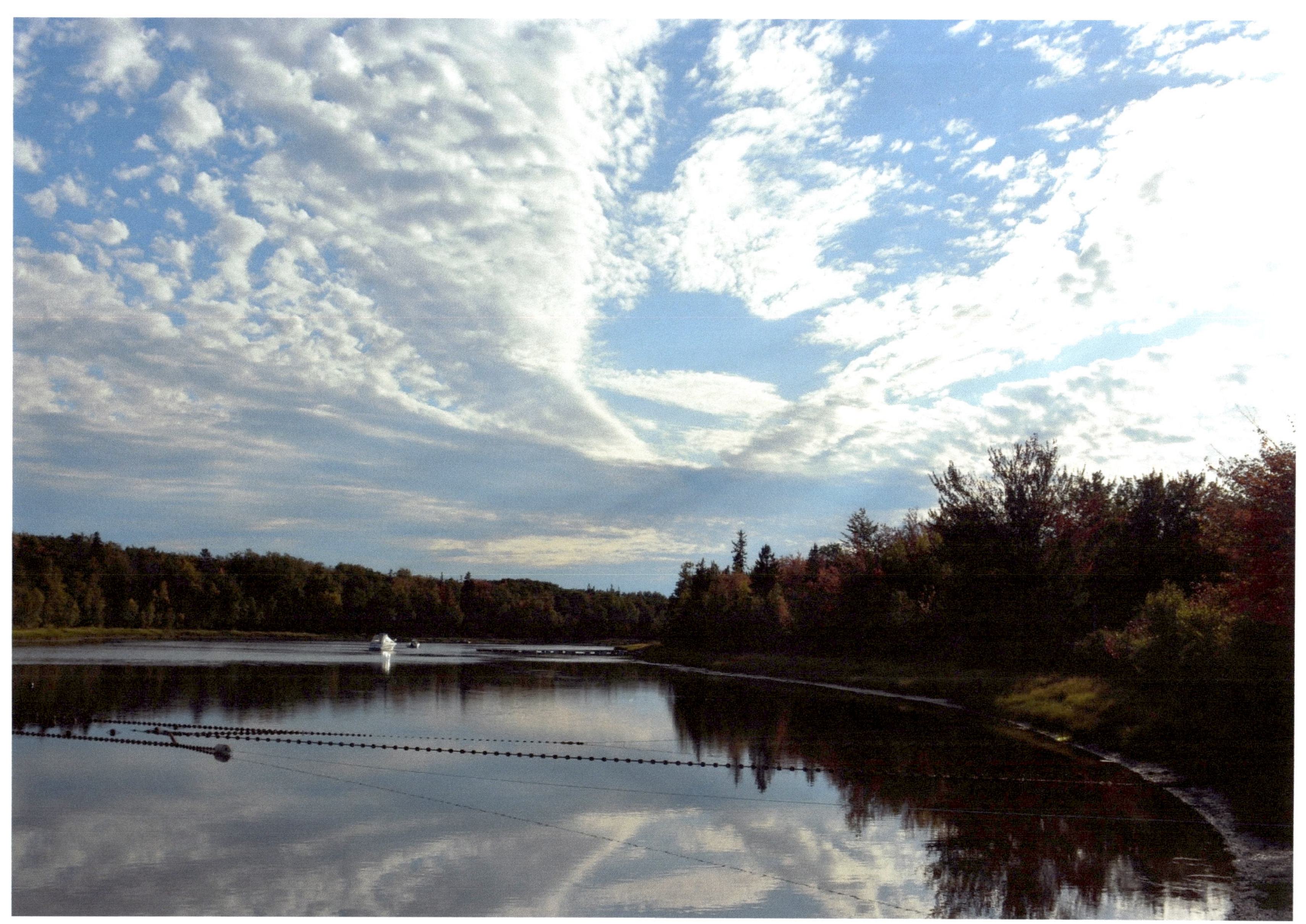

Greek River from Cahoon's Wharf.

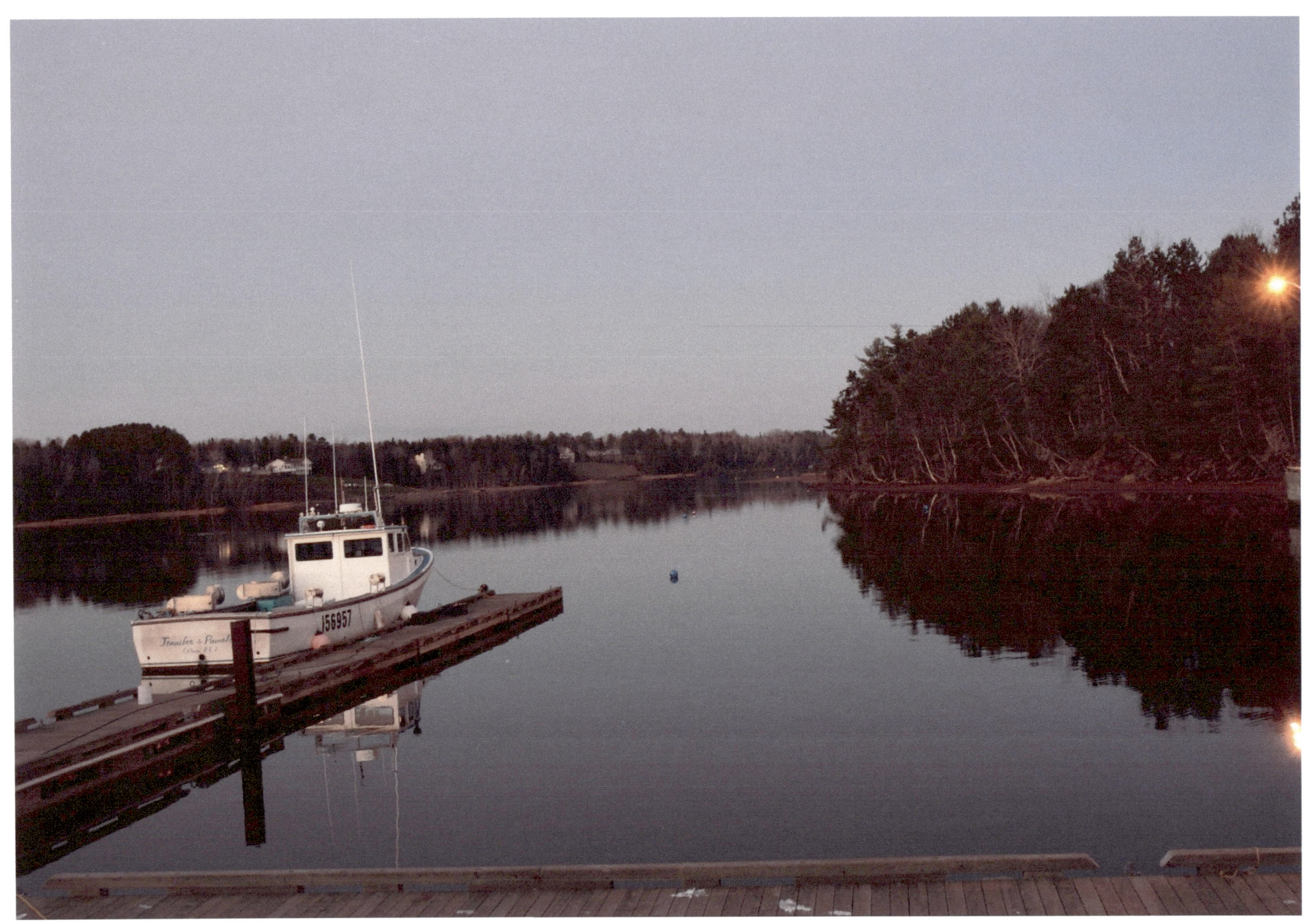

Murray River.

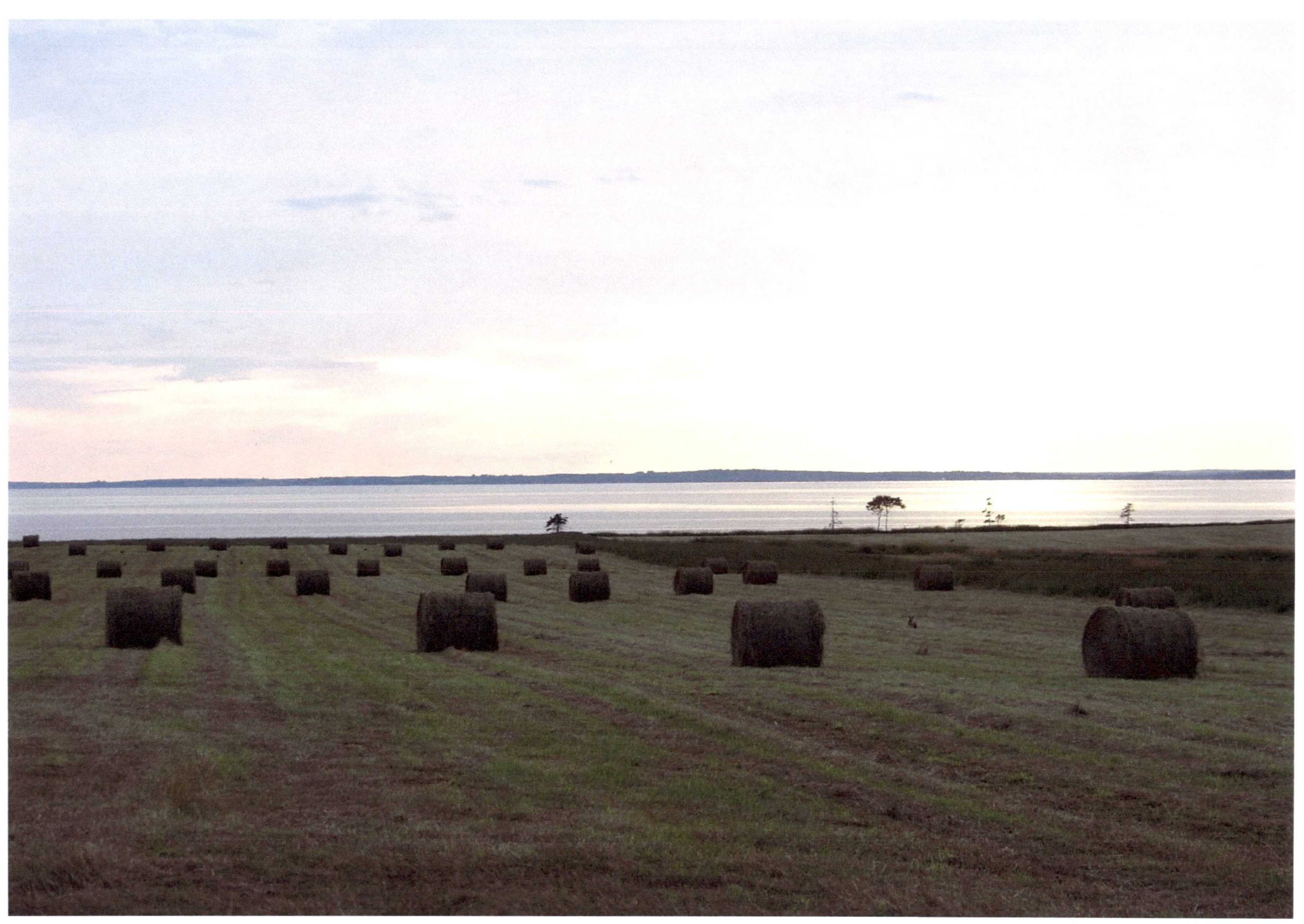

Harvest time overlooking Charlottetown Bay from Earnscliffe .

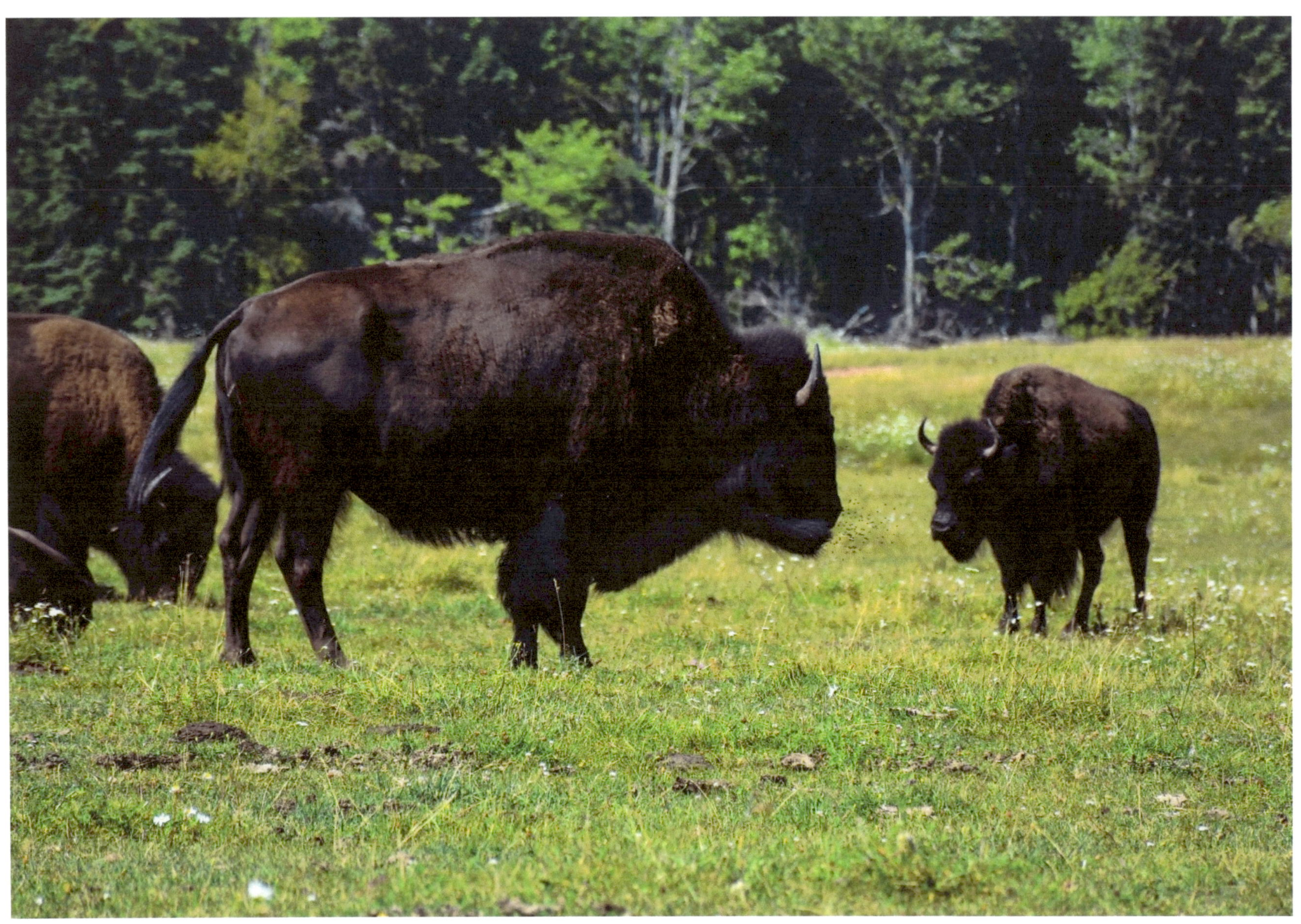

Surprises around every corner, Buffalo herd in the woods.

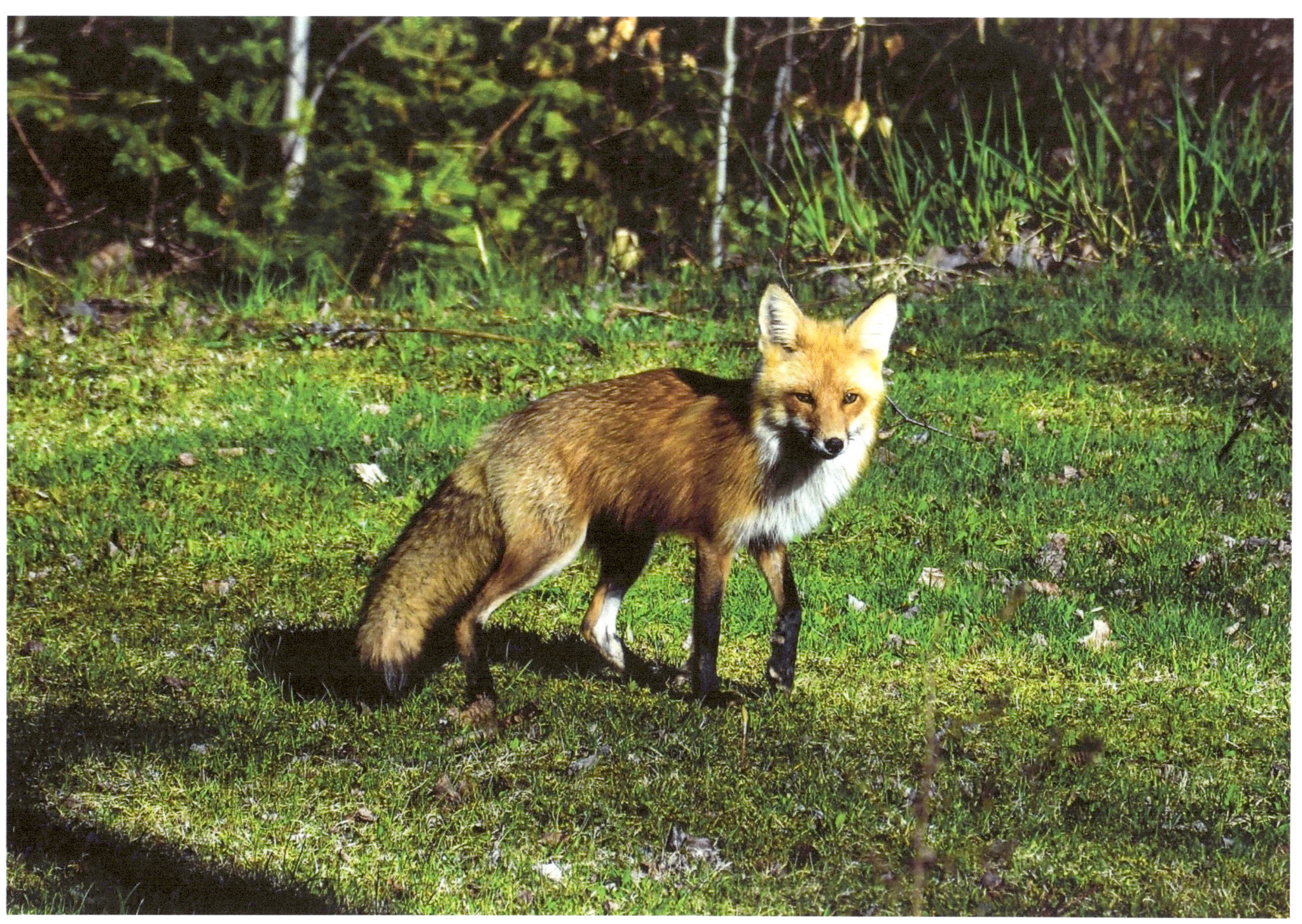

A familiar friend calls back for dinner.

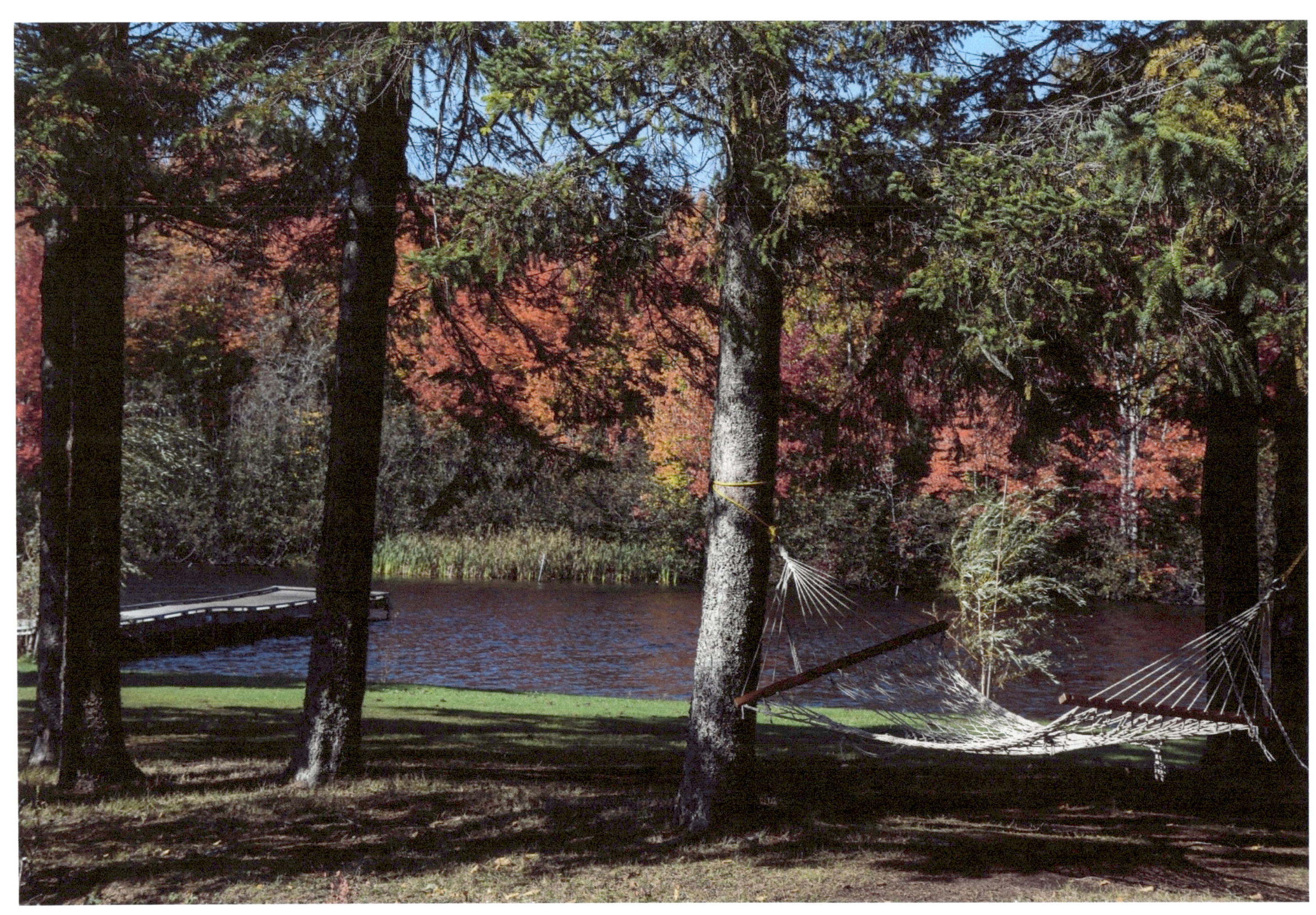

A peaceful spot for a restful afternoon , maybe?

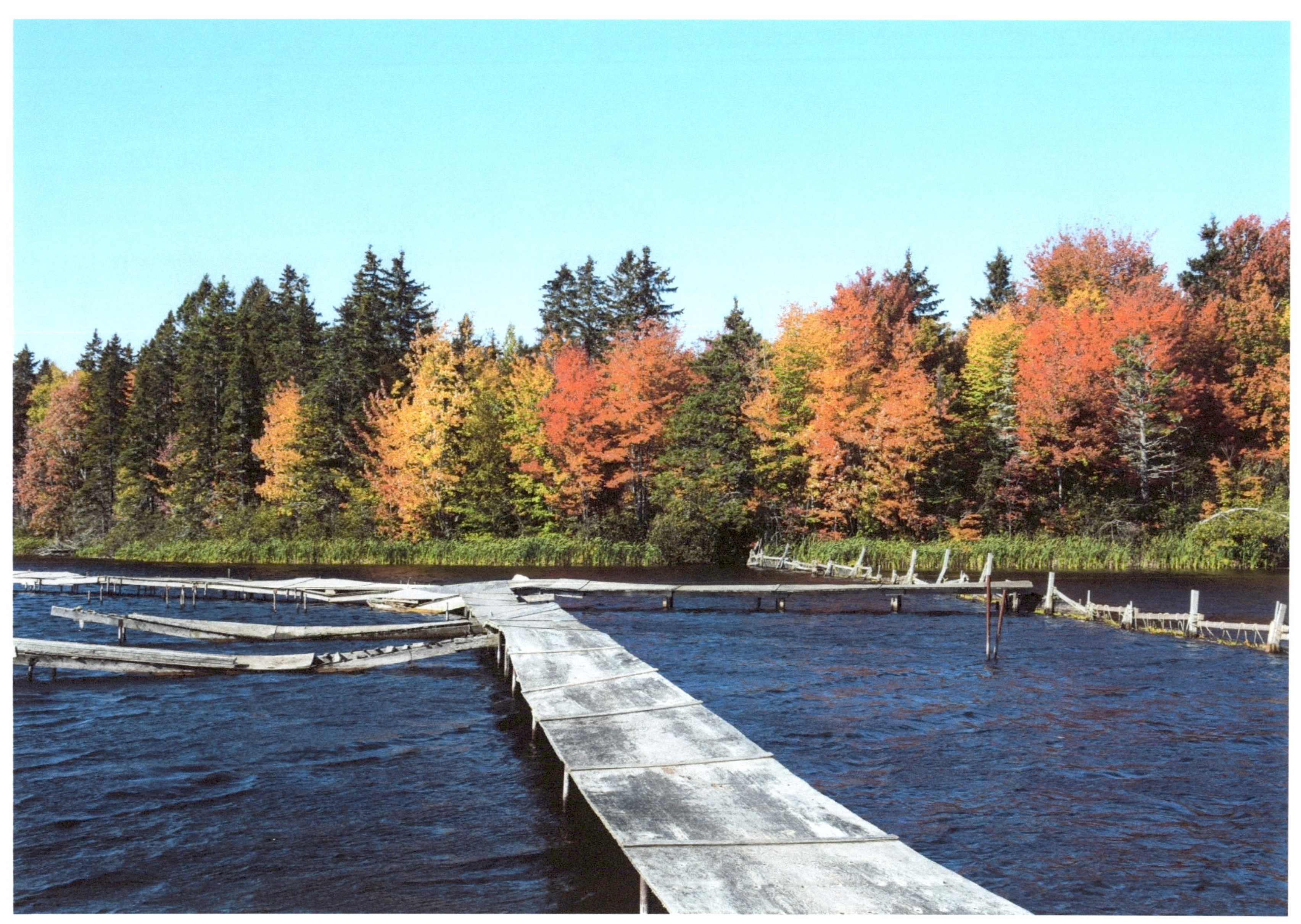

Bens Lake, camp ground and fishing spot.

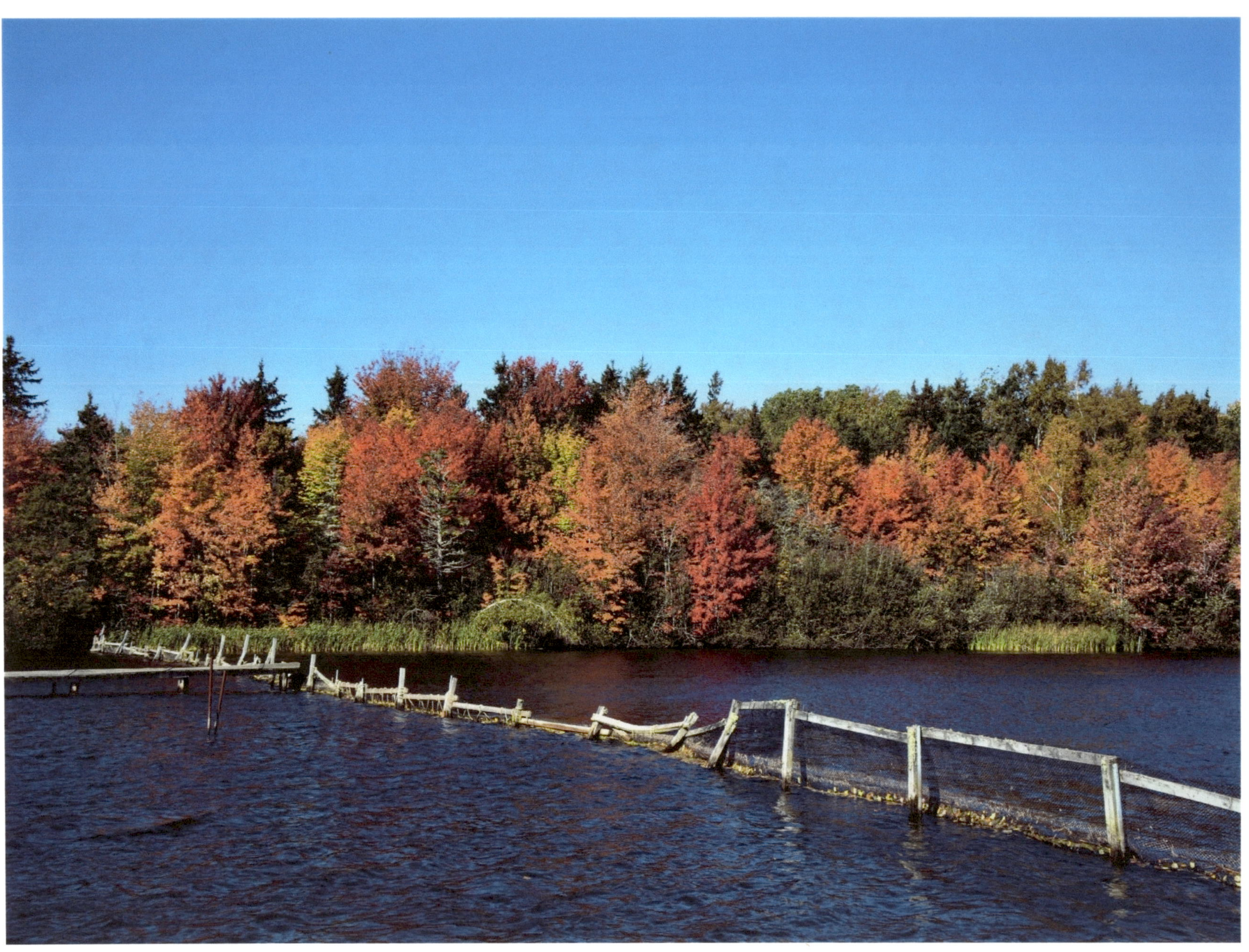

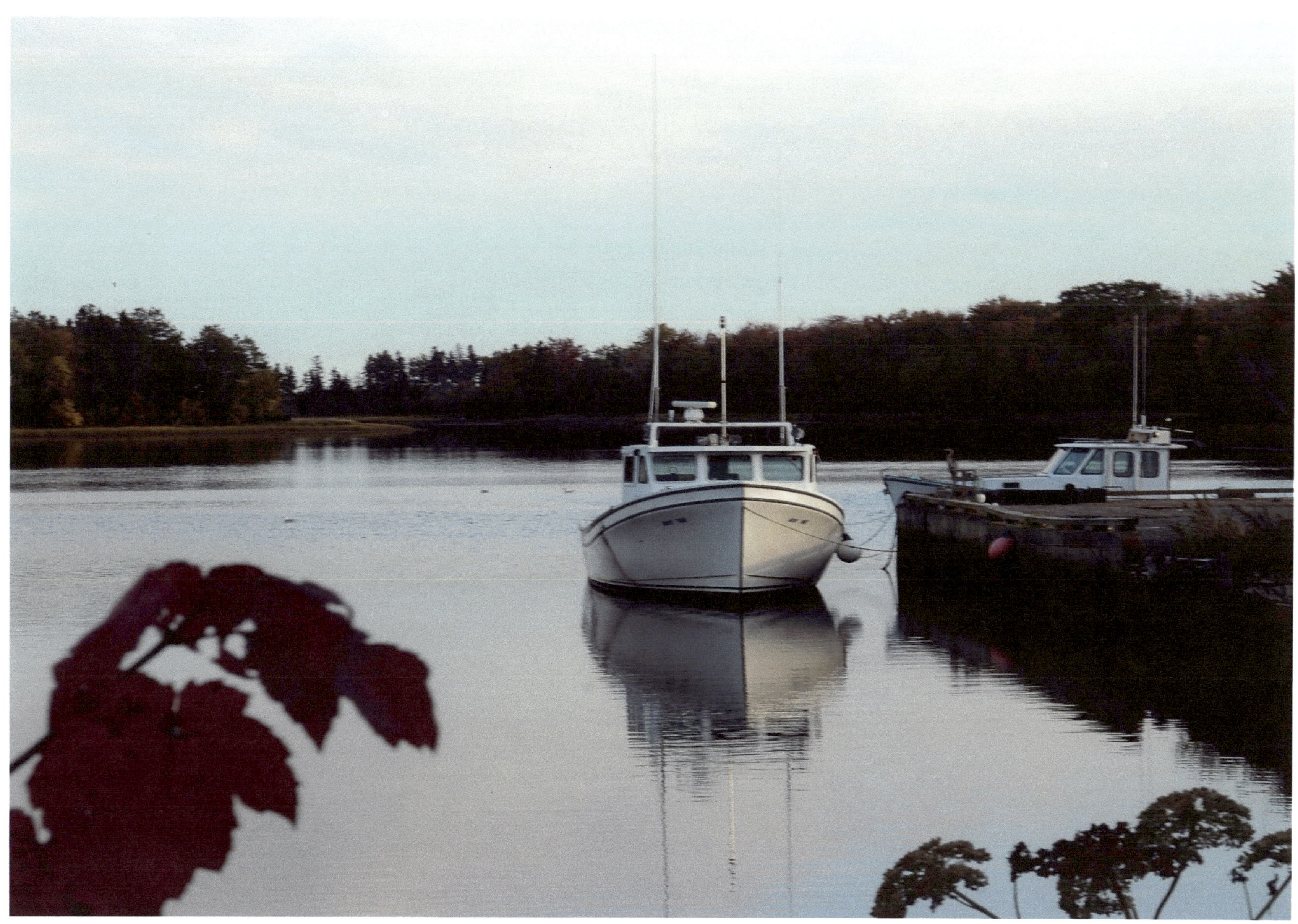

Cahoon's Wharf.

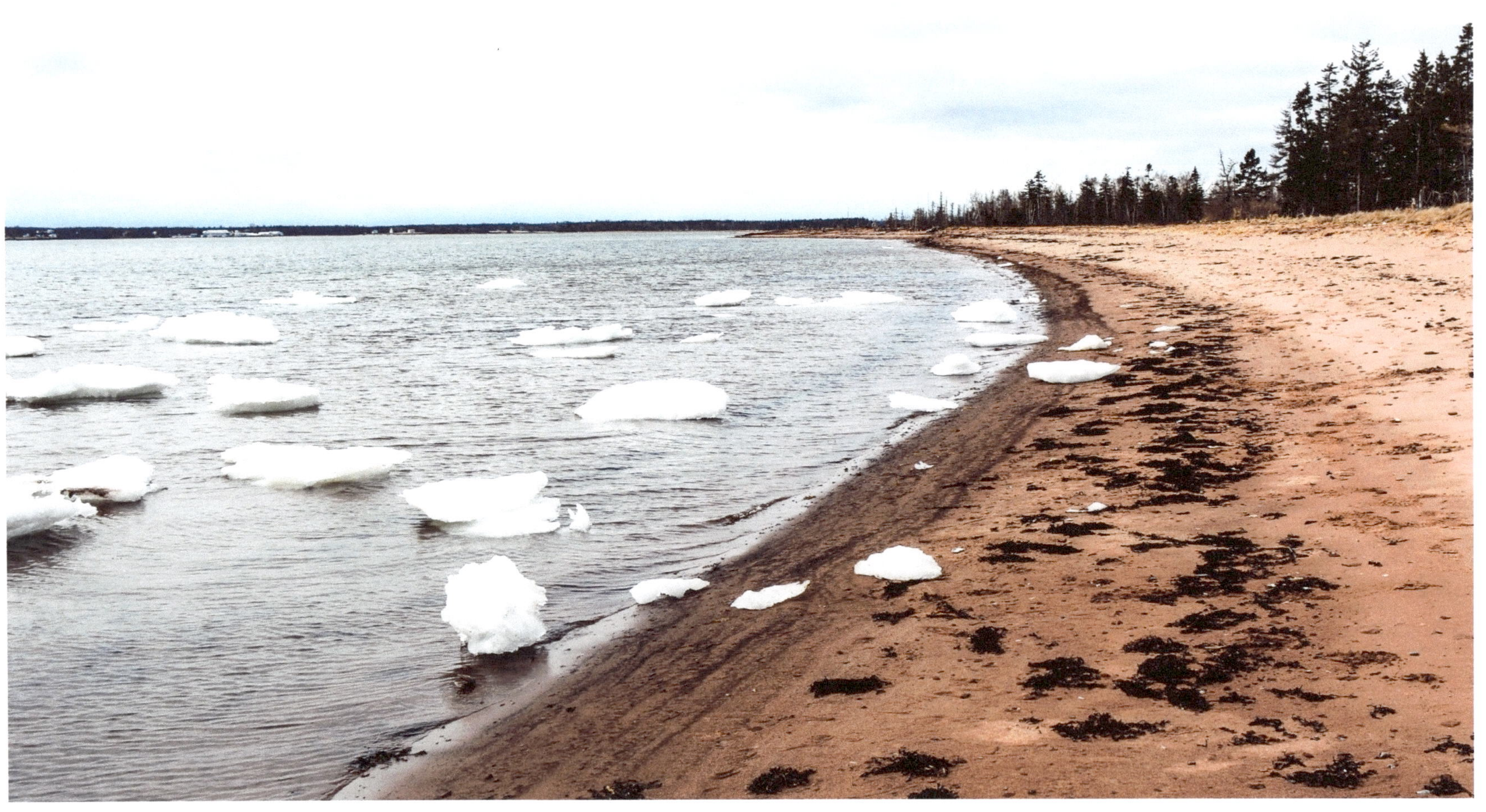

Poverty Beach.

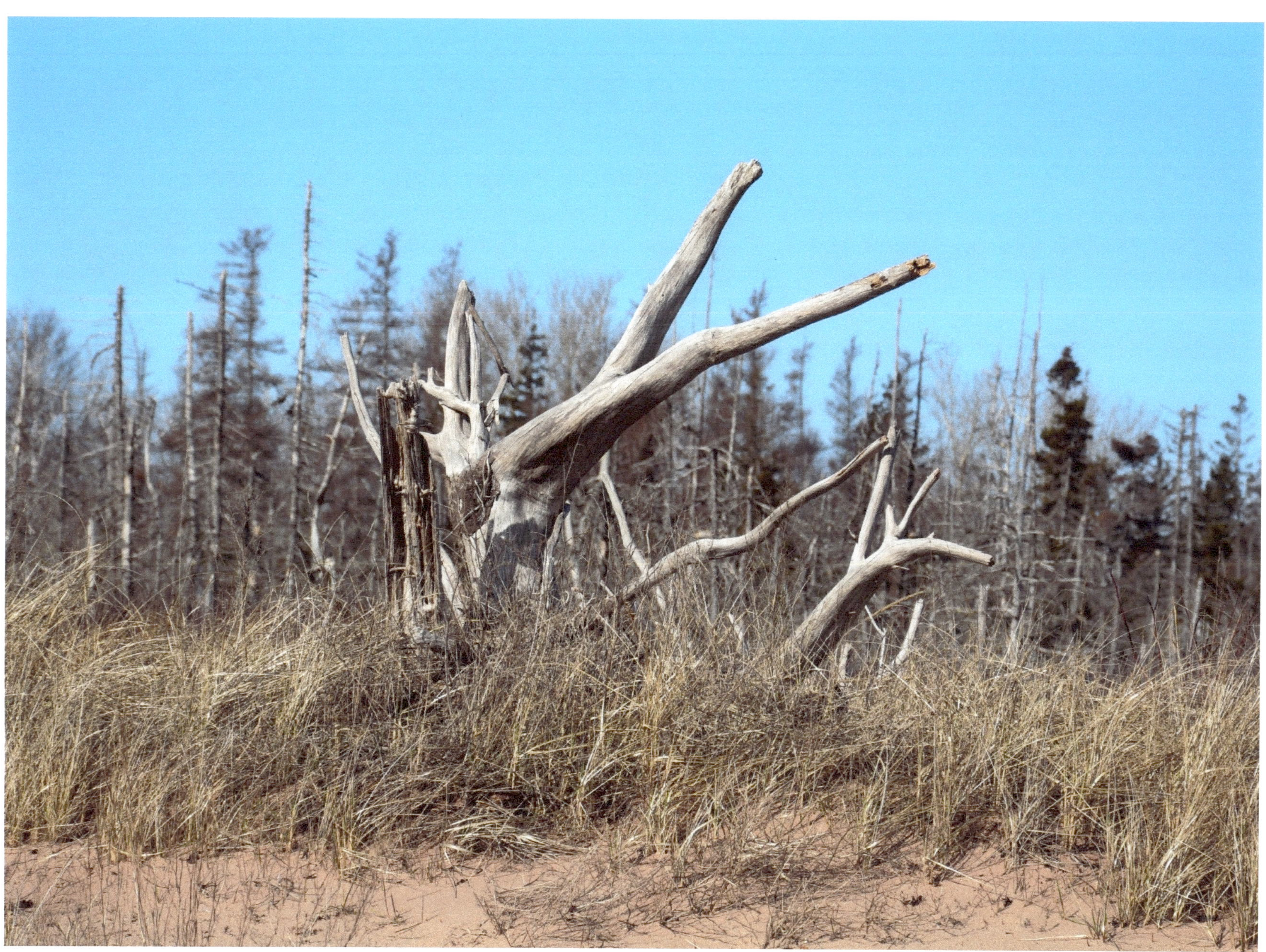

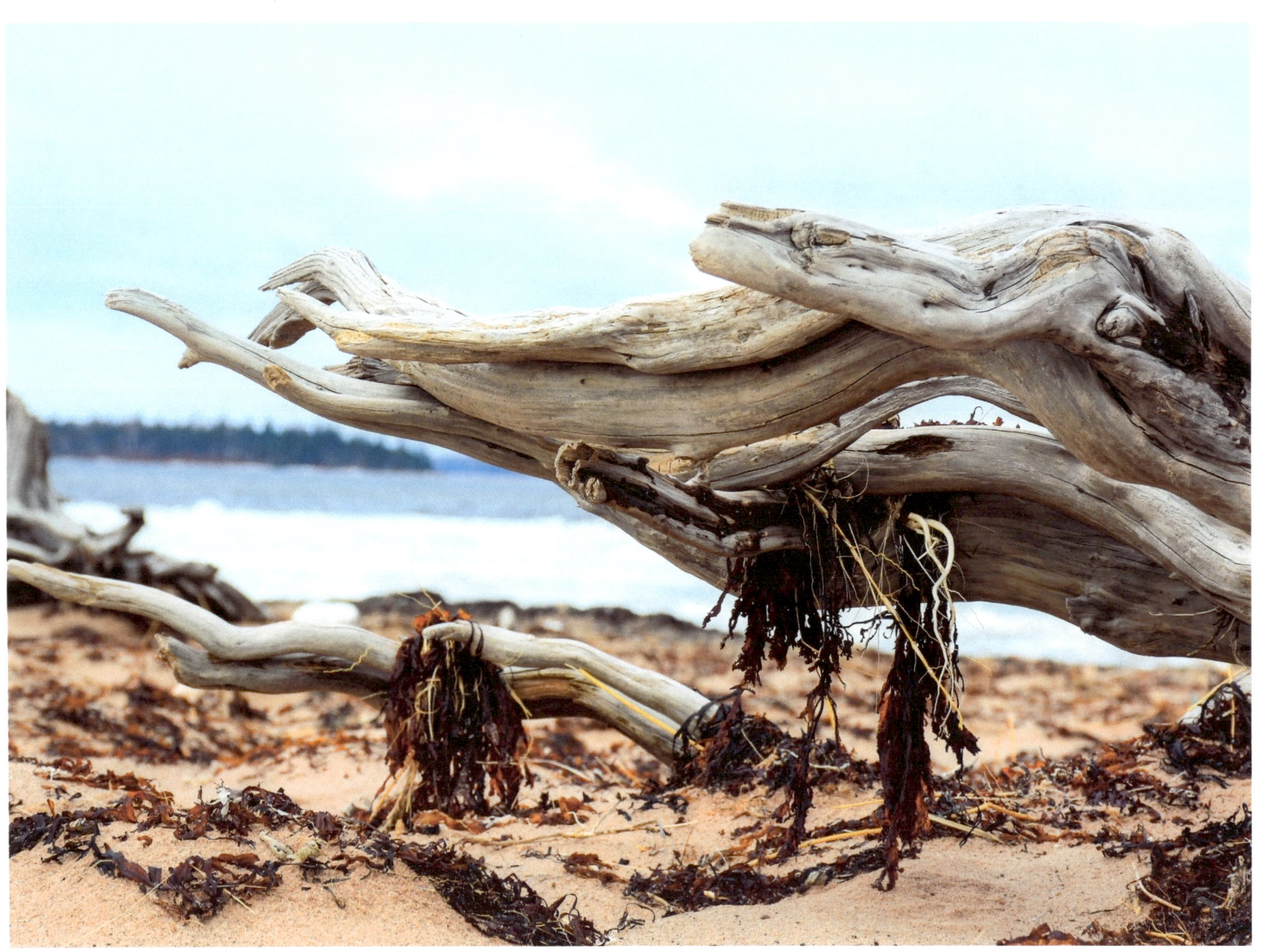

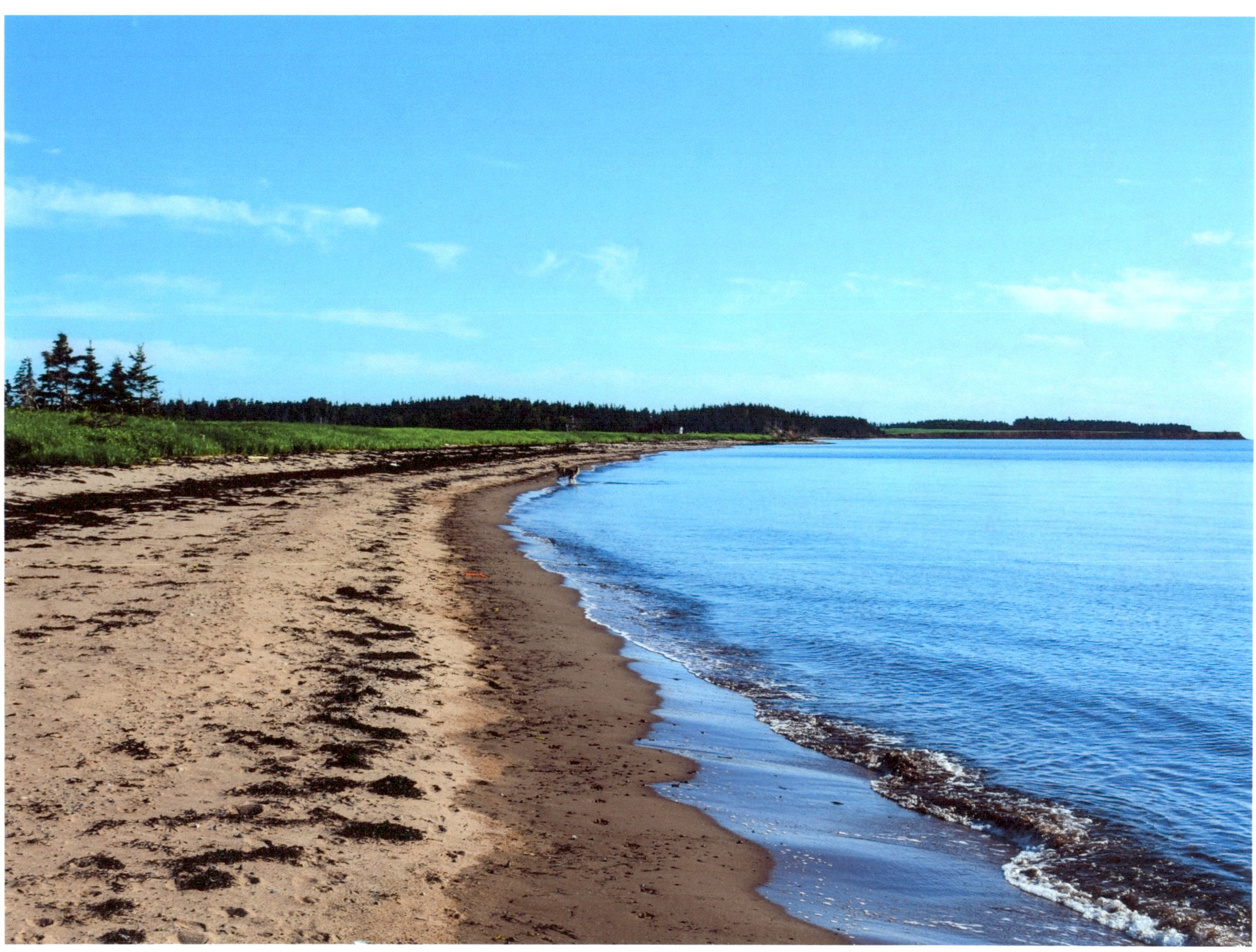

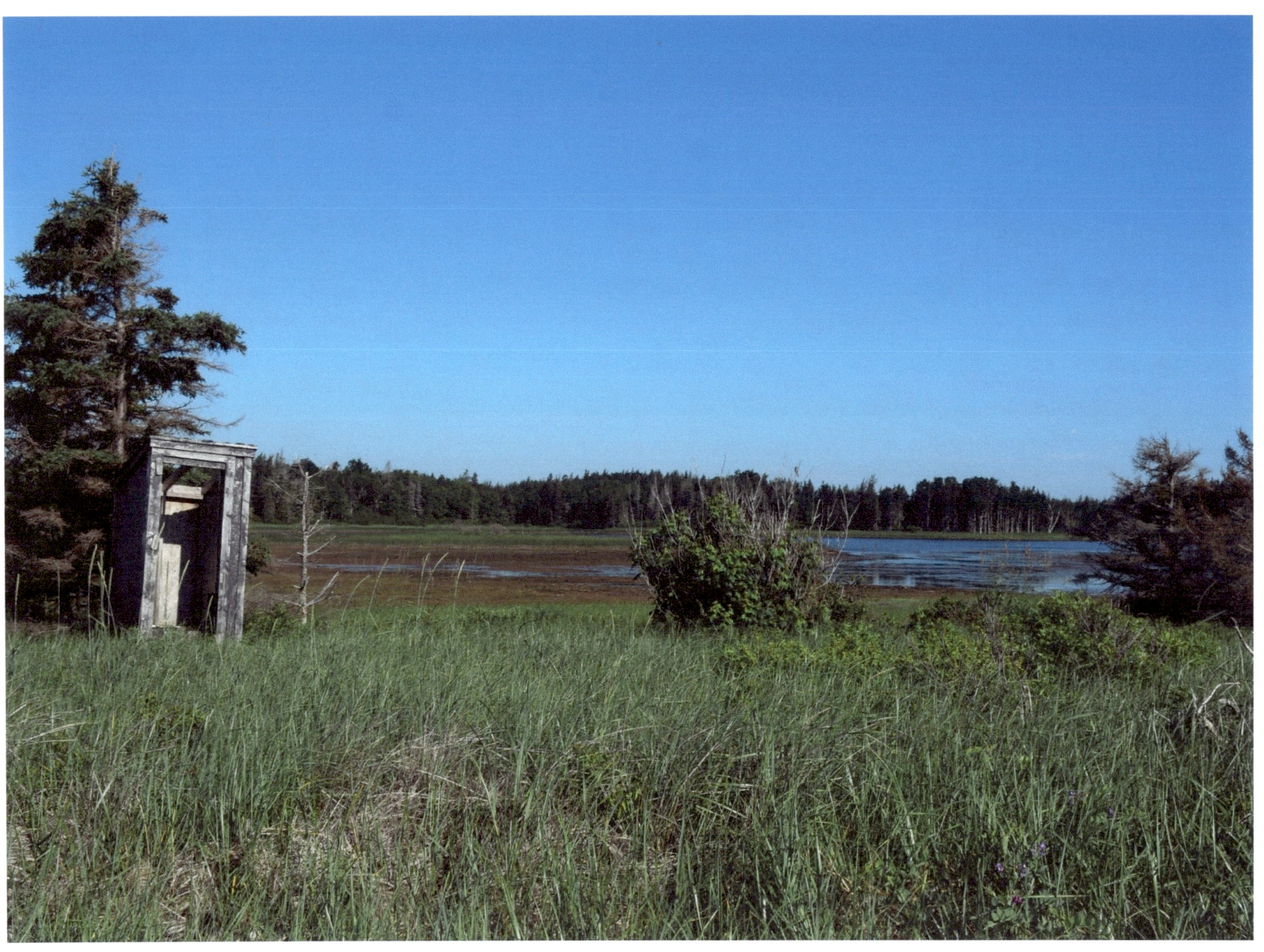

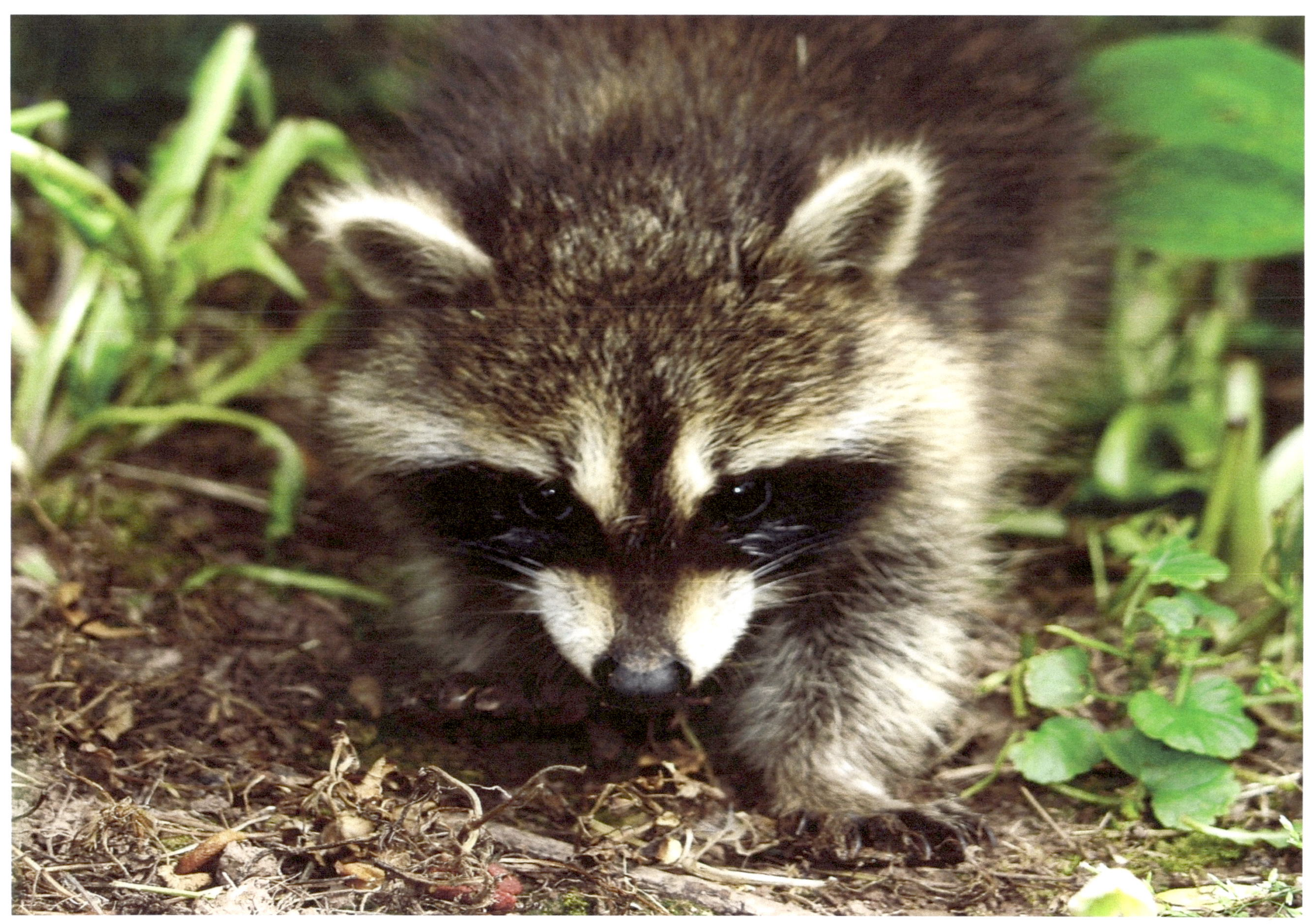

Baby Racoon .

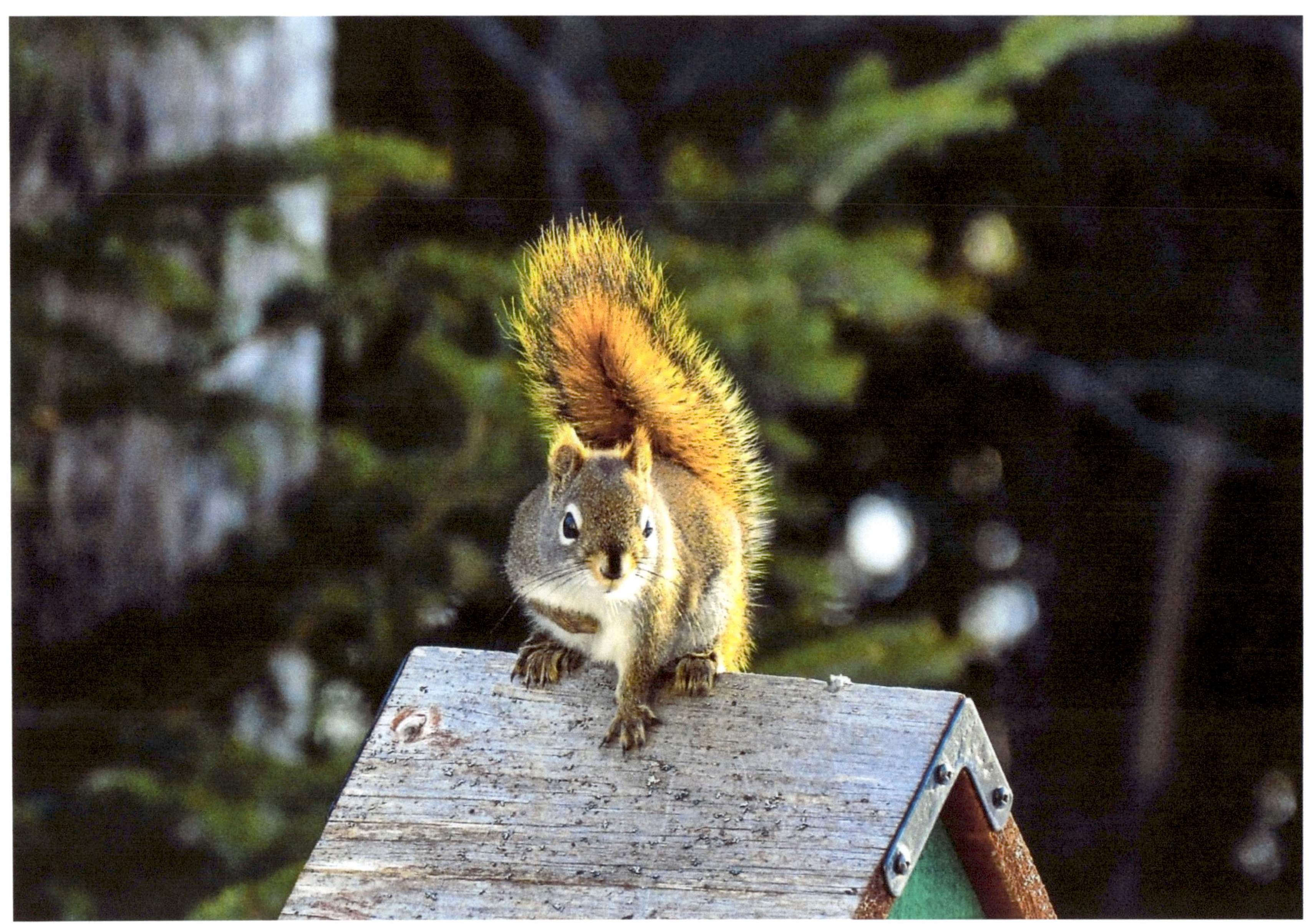

I think he is trying to tell me the bird feeder is empty again!

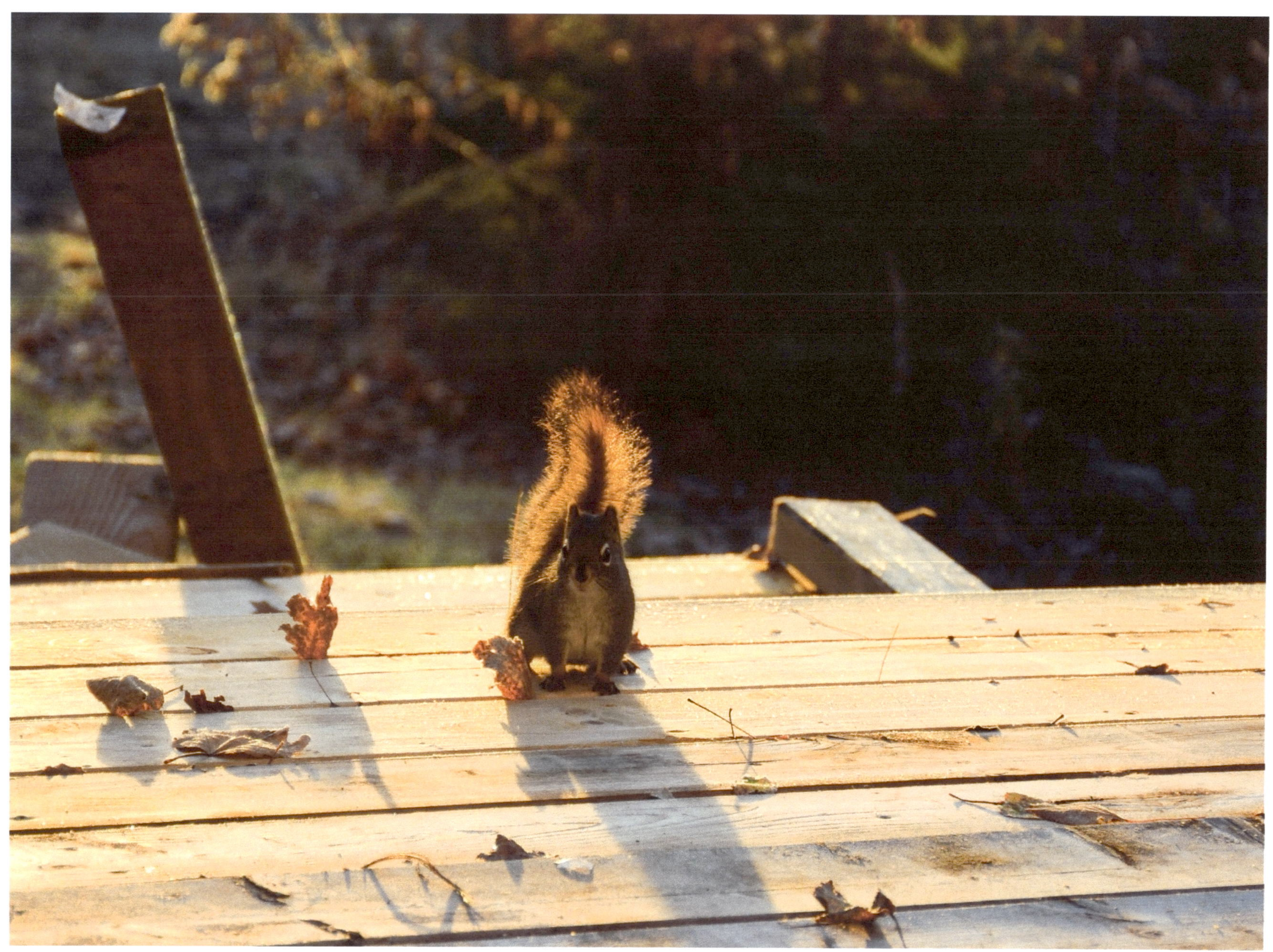

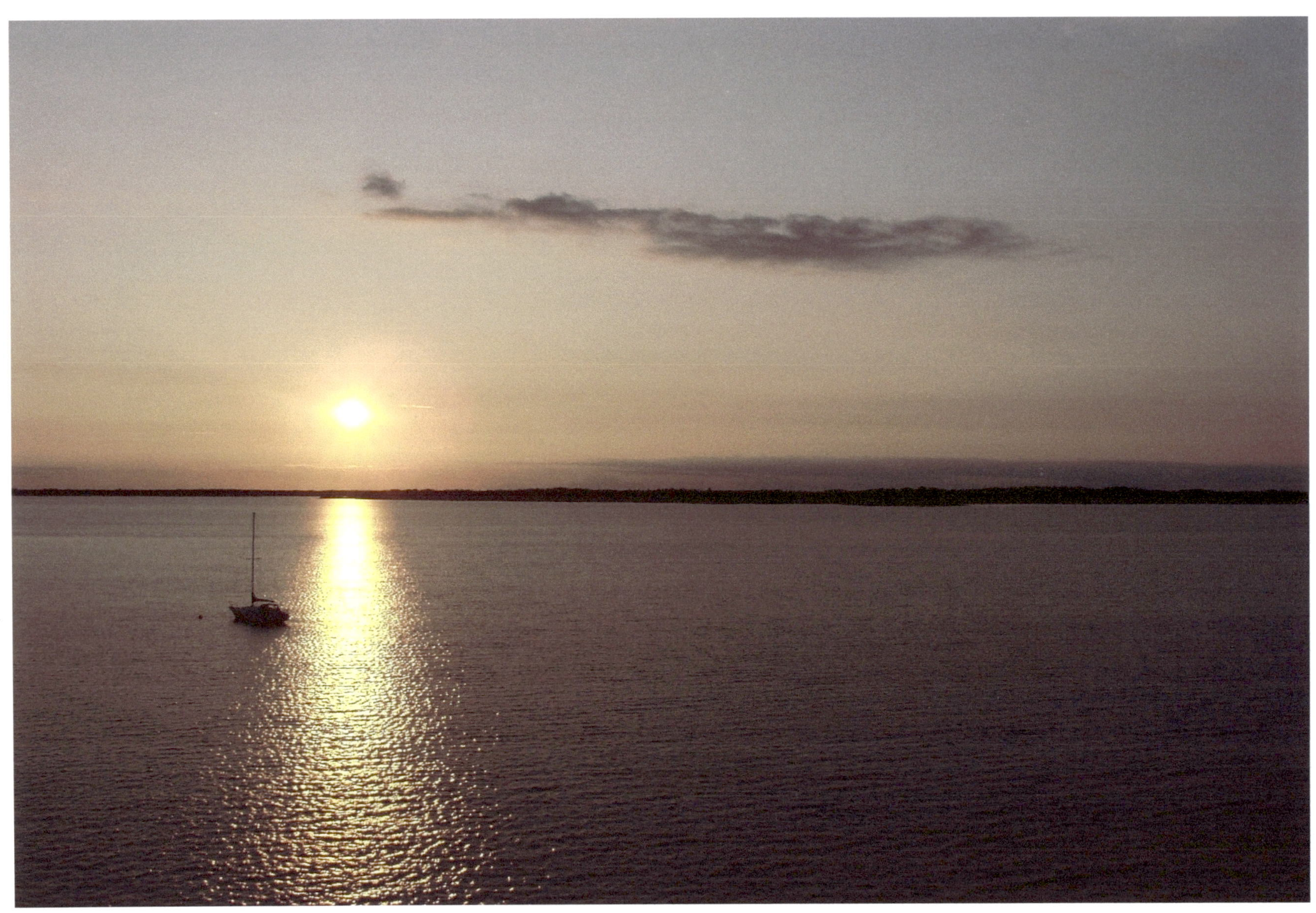

The Northumberland Straight as the sun sets and says good night until tomorrow and then what can we see when a new day begins, over the next hill or around that next corner .

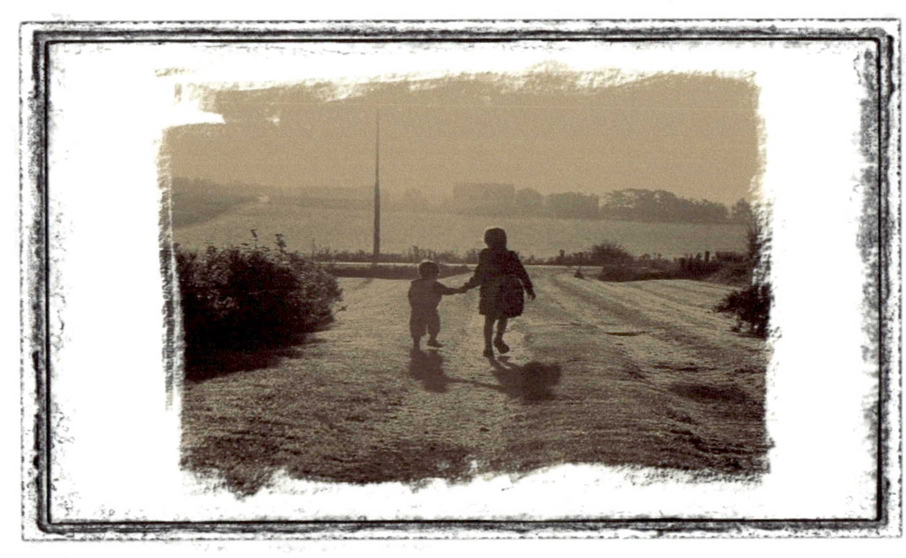

To my two wonderful sons
Kai and Johnny

www.ingramcontent.com/pod-product-compliance
Lightning Source LLC
Chambersburg PA
CBHW042032050726

47599CB00006B/879